The New Normal in Education

The New Normal in Education

Teaching, Learning, and Leading

Mary Beth Klinger and Teresa Coffman

ROWMAN & LITTLEFIELD
Lanham • Boulder • New York • London

Published by Rowman & Littlefield
An imprint of The Rowman & Littlefield Publishing Group, Inc.
4501 Forbes Boulevard, Suite 200, Lanham, Maryland 20706
www.rowman.com

86-90 Paul Street, London EC2A 4NE

Copyright © 2023 by Mary Beth Klinger and Teresa Coffman.

All rights reserved. No part of this book may be reproduced in any form or by any electronic or mechanical means, including information storage and retrieval systems, without written permission from the publisher, except by a reviewer who may quote passages in a review.

British Library Cataloguing in Publication Information Available

Library of Congress Cataloging-in-Publication Data

Names: Klinger, Mary Beth, 1965- author. | Coffman, Teresa, 1966- author.
Title: The new normal in education : teaching, learning, and leading / by Mary Beth Klinger and Teresa Coffman.
Description: Lanham, Maryland : Rowman & Littlefield, [2023] | Includes bibliographical references. | Summary: "This book explores the "new normal" for teaching, learning, and leadership in higher education. Emphasis is placed on welcoming growth and change and being curious to the transformative opportunities that exist for today's students so that the next generation is prepared to solve the world's most pressing issues"— Provided by publisher.
Identifiers: LCCN 2023014492 (print) | LCCN 2023014493 (ebook) | ISBN 9781475867398 (cloth) | ISBN 9781475867404 (paperback: | ISBN 9781475867411 (ebook)
Subjects: LCSH: Education, Higher—Aims and objectives—United States. | Education, Higher—Economic aspects—United States. | Universities and colleges—United States—Faculty. | College students as consumers—United States. | Educational change—United States. | COVID-19 Pandemic, 2020—Influence.
Classification: LCC LA227.4 .K58 2023 (print) | LCC LA227.4 (ebook) | DDC 378.73—dc23/eng/20230608
LC record available at https://lccn.loc.gov/2023014492
LC ebook record available at https://lccn.loc.gov/2023014493

Contents

Preface		vii
Introduction		ix
1	Reimaging Education	1
2	Teaching and Learning	11
3	Instructional Modalities	21
4	Transforming Opportunities for Learning	35
5	Understanding Today's Student	51
6	Collaboration and Community	65
7	Incorporating Inquiry	75
8	Managing in the Post-Pandemic Era	91
9	Leading toward Change	109
10	Reasons for Urgency	119
Bibliography		125
About the Authors		147

Preface

The purpose of this book is to serve as an examination of higher education with regard to teaching, learning, and leading post the COVID-19 pandemic.

Higher education is defined along different continuums and for purposes of this text is considered education beyond K–12 and the receipt of a high school diploma or GED. There are trade schools and apprenticeship programs, community colleges, as well as four-year colleges and universities. The terms college and university are used interchangeably throughout this text.

Education provides a path toward enlightenment, knowledge, and social and economic mobility. This is applied both individually as well as collectively throughout society. It also establishes a democratic citizenship upon which critical debate and discussion can ensue.

Education is connected to higher incomes, better health, and overall happiness. Whether pursued for the distinct purpose of training or for greater knowledge and understanding, the pursuit of life-long learning for wisdom, knowledge, and a voice in our own freedom and choices for the future is inherent in our democratic system.

People of all ages, genders, ethnicities, and socioeconomic backgrounds are motivated to pursue higher education and learning not only for personal gain and achievement but also to apply their new knowledge to communities and for the betterment of society.

Education is often viewed as a bridge to prosperity. The opportunity—through practiced knowledge—to rise from humble backgrounds and achieve greatness in whatever form that is personally or professionally defined.

This book is about hope and opportunity and the future of higher education post-pandemic. While aspects and issues of the past are visited, the emphasis is more on what comes next and the opportunities that await us as we move into this next chapter using educational strategies like collaboration, community, and inquiry.

This book is a joint effort by two career professors in different disciplines and at different institutions of higher education. We relied on our expertise as professors in higher education along with current writings and research on the state of higher education post-pandemic to bring you this text.

Our goal for this book is for you to see the possibilities as well as challenges in the future of education as we move forward for today's students, our communities, and for the whole of higher education.

Introduction

This text serves as a compilation of research, data, and current writings on key issues and concerns around higher education in the United States as of 2023. It addresses the implications of the COVID-19 pandemic, reviews the macroenvironment for higher educational institutions, examines student opportunities, administrative and faculty challenges, and offers suggestions on a path forward for teaching and learning for students, faculty, and institutional leadership.

This book serves as a "snapshot" in time and highlights the changes needed to ensure that educational institutions move nimbly and strategically forward to position their organizations to be responsive to students, affirming to staff and faculty, and partners in the communities they serve.

While there are over four thousand degree-granting institutions of higher education throughout the United States, this text explores the overarching opportunities for the future of these institutions rather than specific details of each.[1]

The real benefit lies with the recommendations and strategic lessons that current and aspiring leaders and faculty within education can use as they navigate the choppy and uncertain landscape of the future of their institutions and higher education in the United States overall.

This book addresses how we can think differently about teaching and learning in higher education. The outline for this text is organized around the future of education from a teaching, learning, and leadership point of view.

Strategies for teaching and learning and the importance of certain critical skills are emphasized to pave the way toward ensuring that our next generation of students are prepared to address the many challenges that lie ahead.

This text examines three key collaborators—educational leaders, faculty, and students. The terms instructor and educator are used interchangeably to refer to faculty at various points throughout the book.

This book explores how we can reengage and reenergize these primary stakeholder groups so we are all "rowing in the same direction" toward student success, employee engagement, and sustainable educational institutions not just for today but for tomorrow as well. This has long-standing implications not just on a micro level for the individual student but on a macro level for the community, the state, the nation, and the world as a whole.

NOTE

1. "Institutions and Programs." U.S. Department of Education, December 3, 2002, https://www2.ed.gov/about/offices/list/ous/international/usnei/us/edlite-institutions-us.html.

Chapter One

Reimaging Education

Education breeds confidence. Confidence breeds hope. Hope breeds peace.

—Confucius, 500 BC

Higher education is embarking upon a new generational learning opportunity. The COVID-19 pandemic has laid bare some of the biggest issues and challenges within higher education, while also availing us to some immense possibilities and opportunities. It truly is the "new normal" as we chart a path forward in teaching, learning, and academic leadership.

Post-pandemic we are exploring new opportunities to positively influence higher education. While teaching strategies and theories for understanding and improving student learning have been in development for hundreds of years, the best ways to teach and learn are continuously a work in progress.

Our vision for higher education is predicated on it serving as a platform upon which new knowledge can spring forth, new innovations can be born, and ultimately stronger communities and societies can be built.

Education is the glue that binds the learning ecosystem to ensure relevant learning. It extends and cultivates student minds beyond the college classroom. Education moves students to become adaptive and flexible so they can transform society toward goals that are sustainable, equitable, and relevant to the current needs of the community.

The response of faculty and educational leaders during this pivotal time in history is imperative to the long-term transformation of teaching and learning. As we make future choices about schooling, we are influencing the experiences of our students and ultimately the investment in society's future.

While there is hope that we have seen the worst of the COVID-19 pandemic, with some of us faring better than others in terms of physical and emotional health for ourselves and our loved ones, the world for the most part seems to be making a valiant effort to move forward. Travel has returned, hospitals have stabilized, and schools have reopened. Masks are optional or nonexistent. Virus rates are high or low or somewhere in between.

Still, at the time of this writing, people continue to lose their lives to COVID-19.[1] Over a million total deaths have been attributed to the pandemic in the United States.[2] Globally, we have lost nearly 7 million people to this disease.[3]

As global leadership guides us through one of the most impactful international health crises of the twenty-first century, we are forever changed. And nowhere is that truer than in education.

We continue to wind our way through the remainder of a 100-year pandemic into the foreseeable future. As we do, many people the world over have a glimmer of optimism that things are improving, and that life as we know it will be filled with more promises and opportunities than it has in the recent past.

We are at a crossroads brought on by the pandemic and our evolving social and cultural times. The question before us is whether we will continue to use the same paradigm that has defined higher education throughout the twenty-first century or whether we will apply what we have learned over the past several years to work more collaboratively and cooperatively to drive learning, resolve inequities, and make a commitment to move forward productively toward real transformational change and progress in higher education.

EVOLUTION OF EDUCATION

The oldest college in the United States is Harvard University founded by John Harvard in 1636.[4] The University of Bologna in Italy, established in 1088, is considered to be the oldest university in the world with the University of Oxford in the United Kingdom not far behind in approximately 1096.[5] Given that formal education has been in existence for nearly a millennium, it is fair to say that education endures.

One of the best outcomes of crisis and change is the opportunity for renewal. Our post-pandemic realities have created tremendous opportunities for reflection, revision, and ultimately growth in higher education.

This is similar to what occurred following the 1918 pandemic when higher education adjusted its practice by increasing collaboration between faculty and staff, as well as engagement within its communities to better serve the public and pursue the goals of education.[6]

In advancing the instructional environment within the classroom, faculty are developing students with a "passion for purpose" and providing them an opportunity to shape their future.

Through education, students are able to meet their life's goals with questions, critical thinking, collaboration, community, and resilience. Institutions of higher education and the classrooms that exist within them, whether fully in-person, hybrid, or fully online, exist as cultural institutions and beacons of engaged communities across the United States and around the world.

ROLE OF EDUCATION

At its heart, the purpose of higher education is about empowering students by providing experiences that develop intellect and expand their knowledge about our changing world, so they have the skills and knowledge to actively challenge and advance society.[7]

The role of education is one that imparts knowledge and prepares students for current realities as well as the world of tomorrow when no one knows exactly what that world will look like. Within higher education, content specific knowledge and technical skills are learned so that students can enter—or retrain for—the world of work.

Importantly, the act of being educated includes active collaboration and engaged participation within the classroom and the college campus so that this can carry over into a career of service within one's community.

Within higher education, students construct meaningful experiences with a diverse student body. They develop critical thinking skills and deeper knowledge and understanding to navigate challenges.

To be educated is to ask questions, and to have the disposition to do so. To realize all of what you do *not* know and be open to learning new things through a process of thinking deeply and critically, and to always consider that learning never ends.[8]

Knowledge extends beyond the constructs of mere understanding to being able to extend learning to communicate clearly, achieve new ways of thinking and understanding, and to develop employable skills that contribute to society and meet an economy's needs.

Education is also about power and rising up to lead when you know the way. This includes the ability to listen to others' views and ideas, and to challenge one's own thinking. Education is a form of social justice whereby you hold yourself as well as others accountable for decisions and actions based on the knowledge you hold and a sense of what is fair and just.[9]

Liberal Arts

The liberal arts include an interdisciplinary curriculum that provides students with diverse skills that they can use to embrace the complexity of a changing society. Along with practical skills and discipline specific knowledge, courses in the liberal arts include subjects such as history, fine arts, religion, science, languages, and literature.

This exposure to a diverse world view within the transformative landscape of learning helps students coexist, negotiate, make decisions, think globally, move toward empathy, and improve their communication with others while also imagining their own future and place in the world.[10]

The liberal arts curriculum helps to develop the critical knowledge and thinking skills that promote adaptability and foster resilience, which are needed to drive one's own learning beyond the classroom. They help to create pathways that connect students to the thinking needed when considering new and emerging challenges and to work collectively to identify solutions to structural problems and creatively shape a new future.[11]

EDUCATION AND CHANGE

Change is defined as making someone or something different, to alter, modify, or reinvent.[12] Educators have witnessed dramatic changes amid tremendous fortitude as they worked through the COVID-19 pandemic. Going forward is the only choice, but whether to do so slow or fast, sideways or straight ahead has remained up for considerable debate.

Effectively managing change requires a transformational approach that is focused on altering the way things are done, while at the same time ensuring stability where and when it is possible. It requires being open and transparent with all stakeholders including those internal to the college or university as well as those that surround and support the institution in the local, state, national, and even global community.

This current period of uncertainty has resulted in some educational leaders placing a wary eye toward the future and what this means for students, teaching, and learning, and ultimately the future of higher education.

Others are inspired and motivated about the challenges presented and the knowledge that education's prowess can move the world and everyone's future in it to a better place given our propensity for innovation, willingness to engage in productive struggle, and our integrity and ethical standards.

As colleges and universities are reevaluating their strategies and the need for change to meet the academic needs of our time, a new generational shift has been emerging in terms of the current Gen Z student, the business approach to academia and the view of "student" as "customer," and the increasing cost of higher education, which has fueled the sentiment that education is a product to be procured.

The goal for leadership in educational institutions today is to manage all these disparate issues and challenges effectively, and through crisis, if need be, while piloting a change effort that will take the institution into the next era.

Leaders are attempting to move the educational institution, its students, employees, and the communities they serve forward in a productive and preemptive manner. Emphasis is placed on being proactive as much as possible and being innovative and creative so that instead of just surviving, the institution is thriving.

EXTERNAL IMPACTS

Beyond the pandemic and over the past several years, we have witnessed unprecedented external influences brought about by political division, economic uncertainties, continued technological advancements, changing cultural norms, and social challenges.

We continue to experience a multitude of issues and conflicts, such as natural disasters, political divisiveness, economic inequality, the spread of misinformation, civil unrest, and continued racial inequities within many communities both in the United States and abroad.[13]

Politics

Politically we continue to try and move toward unity, but many are cynical and cautious as our political leadership struggles to work "across the aisle."[14] As a result, there is an ever-growing skepticism in the United States that has filtrated into classrooms and challenged many of our core democratic values such as truth, honesty, and integrity.[15]

Within education, the goal has been to shape learning, instill values, and guide aspirations while teaching toward an ideal to strengthen and enhance society. The college classroom is a place to engage in discussion and debate around difficult conversations with the goal to create deeper thinking.

This type of thinking and discussion, Aristotle believed, is a method of inquiry that tests both our personal theories and provides opportunities to formulate new understandings in consultation with others so as a community we can solve more complex problems.[16]

On college campuses, there is critical reflection and constructive dialog that connects students' own self-interest to the larger public interest. Evidenced-based knowledge challenges student identities and perspectives with the goal of improving and nourishing our local communities with active and committed citizens skilled in broad democratic competencies.[17]

Economy

The economy continues to amaze, confuse, and remain curious to us all.[18] Whether focused on unemployment, rising and lowering interest rates, inflation, or the stock market, economists and financial experts continue to debate our current economic climate. We continue to see increased division among rich and poor with economic stability and social mobility a major concern.[19]

In terms of the labor market, machines are projected to do half of all work tasks by 2025.[20] Nearly 100 million new roles are expected globally by 2025 as humans, machines, and algorithms learn to work together.[21]

Technology

Technology has changed the way we live and experience the world, and this is only the beginning. Just as we are asking students to think differently about learning with technology, educators are also thinking differently as new and emerging technologies surface throughout education.

Artificial intelligence (AI) is becoming more a part of society. Technologies such as ChatGPT will require that instructors learn to integrate this and other developing technologies into their pedagogy.[22]

This will include teaching students how to think more critically as they research information, ethical use when using AI and other technology tools, seeking out ways to critically present information, and the potential limitations as well as strengths of various technology tools.[23]

As new technologies come onboard, educators actively seek ways to personalize student learning. For example, by utilizing real-world simulations designed to create authentic opportunities to learn by questioning, communicating with outside experts, and analyzing the use of a variety of resources in new and meaningful ways.

Online learning has blossomed in popularity, especially among students who need flexibility and are juggling multiple priorities like work and family.[24] Technology integration in the classroom, whether face-to-face, virtual, or hybrid is now commonplace with course management systems and the Internet.

Culture

Colleges traditionally have shared beliefs, customs, and a history that connects the institution and its community together. After working remotely during the pandemic, members of the educational community are now back on campus working post-pandemic to reestablish a positive and shared culture among students, faculty, and staff with a renewed awareness on assimilating diverse cultures and experiences back into the campus community.[25]

Some schools are updating and redefining their vision and mission statements post-pandemic. More inclusive activities are being offered to engage more directly and intimately with students to reconnect them to the college community and its shared values while recognizing students' unique experiences and how they add to the learning environment.[26]

Social

Within education, we are troubled about students and a potential future generation who have disappeared from the classroom and wonder where these students have gone.[27] Students who have dropped out—even temporarily—are at great risk of not returning. Of the 2.6 million students who began college in fall 2019, over 25 percent or close to seven hundred thousand students did not return in fall 2020.[28]

Low-income students struggled to afford college, housing, and food throughout the pandemic. Homelessness and housing insecurity have been a persistent issue.[29] During 2020, 14 percent of students experienced homelessness while over 40 percent were housing insecure, and during this same year, over 38 percent of college students were food insecure.[30] Access to affordable childcare for today's college student has also been a challenge.[31]

Many colleges and universities are working to provide students with resources, such as alternative living arrangements, food pantries, childcare, and clothing. Legislation has been introduced in the U.S. Congress, titled the Housing for Homeless Students Act of 2022, to allow current or formally homeless students to live in low-income properties near their campus.[32]

Faculty are also finding ways to support students in their classes by facilitating a greater sense of belonging and addressing individual learning needs. This fosters comradery, collaboration, and cooperation.

The increased personalization and social engagement incorporated into the learning process creates an opportunity-centered teaching approach. One focused on establishing relationships, community building, identity development, self-determination, and intent on seeing a student's well-being as the foundation of learning prior to adding in specific content knowledge.[33]

MOVING FORWARD

Given the current challenges and struggles, there is a better way forward post-pandemic and higher education can lead the way as we navigate the internal landscape, external forces, and the role of education for society in meeting the needs of the next generation.[34]

Colleges and universities will continue to effectively prepare students by instilling knowledge as well as new ideas and possibilities that will continue to change and advance our world.

Our educational system is predicated on building knowledge, increasing learning, and supporting growth so individuals can improve their lives through employment, entrepreneurship, and service, and advance not just the political, economic, technological, cultural, and social efforts of a nation, but the world as a whole.

The goals for higher education for the remainder of the twenty-first century endure. They are central and critical to the advancement of a global society where we live and exchange knowledge and ideas.

Just like those before us, we continue to build a global community and a future that acknowledges and embraces change and evolution. We are developing in students both competence and ability, along with trust, integrity, honesty, and a commitment to democratic principles that support universal ideals.

NOTES

1. "COVID-19 Mortality Overview," CDC National Center for Health Statistics 2022, https://www.cdc.gov/nchs/covid19/mortality-overview.htm.

2. "COVID-19 Data Review: Update on COVID-19–Related Mortality," Centers for Disease Control and Prevention, January 15, 2023, https://www.cdc.gov/coronavirus/2019-ncov/science/data-review/index.html.

3. "WHO Coronavirus (COVID-19) Dashboard," World Health Organization, 2023, https://covid19.who.int/.

4. Mark Abad and Erin McDowell, "The Oldest College in Every US State," *Business Insider*, 2018, https://www.businessinsider.com/oldest-college-every-state-2018-10.

5. Laura T. "10 of the Oldest Universities in the World," Top Universities.com, December 2022, https://www.topuniversities.com/blog/10-oldest-universities-world.

6. Genevieve Carlton, "Higher Education and Pandemics," Best Colleges, May 11, 2022, https://www.bestcolleges.com/blog/higher-education-and-pandemics/.

7. "The Purpose of Higher Education Part 1," The Change Leader, January 24, 2023, https://changinghighered.com/the-purpose-of-higher-education-part-1/.

8. John Dewey, *Experience and Education* (Toronto: Collier-MacMillan Canada Ltd. 1938).

9. Brenda Álvarez, "Why Social Justice in School Matters," NeaToday, January 22, 2019, https://www.nea.org/advocating-for-change/new-from-nea/why-social-justice-school-matters.

10. Andrew McKie, "Using the Arts and Humanities to Promote a Liberal Nursing Education: Strengths and Weaknesses," *Nurse Education Today* 32, no. 7. (2012): 803–10.

11. James Buckwalter-Arias, "Liberal Education After the Pandemic," American Association of University Professors, Fall 2020, https://www.aaup.org/article/liberal-education-after-pandemic#.Y8QjG-zMKRw.

12. Merriam-Webster Dictionary, "Change," 2022, https://www.merriam-webster.com/dictionary/change.

13. Janna Anderson, Lee Raine, and Emily A. Vogels, "Experts Say the 'New Normal' in 2025 Will Be Far More Tech-Driven, Presenting More Big Challenges," Pew Research Center, February 18, 2021, https://www.pewresearch.org/internet/2021/02/18/experts-say-the-new-normal-in-2025-will-be-far-more-tech-driven-presenting-more-big-challenges/.

14. Jim Tankersley and Alan Rappeport, "America Hit Its Debt Limit, Setting Up Bitter Fiscal Fight," *The New York Times,* January 19, 2023, https://www.nytimes.com/2023/01/19/us/politics/debt-limit-economy.html.

15. "In Views of U.S. Democracy, Widening Partisan Divides over Freedom to Peacefully Protest," Pew Research Center, September 2, 2020, https://www.pewresearch.org/politics/2020/09/02/in-views-of-u-s-democracy-widening-partisan-divides-over-freedom-to-peacefully-protest/.

16. Terence Irwin, "Inquiry and Dialectic," in *Aristotle's First Principles* (Oxford Academic, 1990): 26–50.

17. Sjur Bergan, "How Universities Can Promote 'Democratic Competences' Among Students," Times Higher Education, March 24, 2022, https://www.timeshighereducation.com/campus/how-universities-can-promote-democratic-competences-among-students.

18. Naim Moises, "Fads and Fashion in Economic Reforms: Washington Consensus or Washington Confusion?" International Monetary Fund, October 26, 1999, https://www.imf.org/external/pubs/ft/seminar/1999/reforms/naim.htm.

19. Juliana Menasce Horowitz, Ruth Igielnik, and Rakesh Kochhar, "Trends in Income and Wealth Inequality," Pew Research Center, January 9, 2020, https://www.pewresearch.org/social-trends/2020/01/09/trends-in-income-and-wealth-inequality/.

20. "Machines to 'Do Half of All Work Tasks By 2025,'" BBC, October 21, 2020, https://www.bbc.com/news/business-54622189.

21. Victoria Masterson, "From Medicine Drones to Coral Cleaners: 3 'Jobs of The Future' That Are Already Here," World Economic Forum, May 25, 2022, https://www.weforum.org/agenda/2022/05/robots-help-humans-future-jobs/.

22. Patrick Wood and Mary Louise Kelly, 'Everybody Is Cheating': Why This Teacher Has Adopted an Open ChatGPT Policy," National Public Radio, January 26, 2023, https://www.npr.org/2023/01/26/1151499213/chatgpt-ai-education-cheating-classroom-wharton-school.

23. Brian Alexander, "What Might ChatGPT Mean for Higher Education?" YouTube, https://youtu.be/Bz7aW6vStBw.

24. "CHLOE 7: Tracking Online Learning from Mainstream Acceptance to Universal Adoption: The Changing Landscape of Online Education," *Encoura,* 2022, https://encoura.org/project/chloe-7/.

25. "Building the Future of Education," OECD, 2023, https://www.oecd.org/education/future-of-education-brochure.pdf.

26. Alyssa M. Lederer, Mary T. Hoban, Sarah K. Lipson, Sasha Zhou, and Daniel Eisenberg, "More Than Inconvenienced: The Unique Needs of U.S. College Students during the COVID-19 Pandemic," *Pandemic Health Education & Behavior* 48, no. 1 (2020): 14–19.

27. "UNESCO COVID-19 Education Response: How Many Students Are at Risk of Not Returning to School? Advocacy Paper," UNESCO: United Nations Educational Scientific and Cultural Organization, 2020.

28. Matt Krupnick, "More Students Are Dropping Out of College during COVID—And It Could Get Worse," The Hechinger Report, February 10, 2022, https://hechingerreport.org/more-students-are-dropping-out-of-college-during-covid-and-it-could-get-worse/.

29. Stefanos Chen, "A New Lifeline for the Unseen: Homeless College Students.," *The New York Times*, December 2022, https://www.nytimes.com/2022/12/18/realestate/college-housing-homeless-students.html.

30. "#Realcollege 2021: Basic Needs Insecurity during the Ongoing Pandemic," The Hope Center, March 31, 2021, https://hope.temple.edu/sites/hope/files/media/document/HopeNationalReport2021-22-compressed-compressed.pdf.

31. Brittani Williams, Jinann Bitar, Portia Polk, Andre Nguyen, Gabriel Montague, Carrie Gillispie, Antoinette Waller, Azeb Tadesse, and Kayla Elliott, "Student Parent Affordability," *The Education Trust*, August 2022, https://edtrust.org/wp-content/uploads/2014/09/For-Student-Parents-The-Biggest-Hurdles-to-a-Higher-Education-Are-Cost-and-Finding-Child-Care-August-2022.pdf.

32. 117th U.S. Congress. *S.5108—Housing for Homeless Students Act of 2022*, Washington, DC: U.S. Congress.

33. Justin Reich, "To Serve All of Our Students, 'We have to do something differen,t'" EdSurge, January 2023, https://www.edsurge.com/news/2023-01-10-to-serve-all-of-our-students-we-have-to-do-something-different.

34. "Building the Future of Education," OECD, 2023.

Chapter Two

Teaching and Learning

The best teachers are those who show you where to look, but don't tell you what to see.

—Alexandra K. Trenfor

The need for emergency remote teaching due to the COVID-19 pandemic resulted in dramatic alternations to teaching and learning over the past several years. As colleges and universities returned to in-person instruction the transformation has continued as educators strive to bring about deeper and more meaningful learning for today's student.[1]

According to the U.S. Department of Education, the instructional environment encompasses the behavioral, instructional, and personal aspects of the classroom experience.[2] Quality teaching tops the list. Educators are subject-matter experts in their field. They consider how to take their specialized knowledge and expertise and disseminate it in meaningful ways to influence student learning most effectively.[3]

For faculty, questions about how best to motivate and present discipline-specific content, provide feedback, check for understanding, and work most successfully with students are key topics of today. Educators are listening intently to their students, colleagues, and the broader community to modify and adapt their teaching practices to meet student needs.[4]

The instructional environment is more than the classroom. It is an entire college or university experience. For many students, the act of being immersed in higher education is transformational in terms of not only faculty-to-student interactions, but also in the growth and development that results from student-to-student discussions held in class, dormitories, dining halls, and throughout the college campus and at a variety of college events.

In addition to faculty, other employees throughout the university play a key role in student development whether it is through the residence halls, advising, career services, or financial aid, to name a few. Every interaction and touch point that the student has within the educational institution is of significance.

These positive interactions and opportunities for engagement, especially after emergency remote learning, foster student confidence, engagement, and community.[5] Students feel as though they belong within the institution and are supported as they develop intellectually, emotionally, socially, and spiritually through and within their higher education community.

Learning is transformational and life changing. Higher education brings with it opportunities, decisions, and outcomes that did not exist previously. Ultimately, the pursuit of a course, program, or degree has the potential to positively change a student's life in ways that the graduating senior could not have comprehended at the start of their educational journey.

TEACHING TWENTY-FIRST CENTURY SKILLS

There are critical skills needed by students to be successful in today's world. They have remained relatively constant over time, even amidst continuous change, and have endured in serving students well.

Soft skills, or what some have termed "twenty-first-century skills," include critical and creative thinking, collaboration and team building, synthesis and analysis, as well as opportunities for reflection and contemplation to help develop a lifelong learner mindset and to meet challenges more confidently and expertly.

Learning, literacy, and life skills are the three main categories needed by today's graduates in a world where change is nonstop and learning is continuous.[6]

- *Learning skills* teach students about the mental processes needed within the world of work and include critical thinking, creativity, collaboration, and communication.
- *Literacy skills* focus on students' ability to understand facts and separate truth from fiction when using different sources of information, media, and technology.
- *Life skills* ask students to develop personally and professionally in ways that will benefit them for career readiness, such as flexibility, leadership, initiative, productivity, and social skills.[7]

These twenty-first century skills prepare and instill confidence in students to be enthusiastic participants within a global society. They facilitate the development of a worldview by exposing students to diverse viewpoints.[8] They help students develop empathy and understanding as they engage within their communities, and they empower students to feel courageous and serve as forces of change.

While higher education facilitates the development of these skills that both prepare students to think as well as for preparation in the world of work, it is not a one-size-fits-all approach. Rather it is a compilation of developing the mind, social, and individual competencies, along with an ability to interact, think, and create that ultimately advances not just the instructional environment but the students themselves.

Learning, discovery, attempting, and creating are all part of the educative process. Together they offer an integrated approach. There is both a personal and social need to understand.

Education must be sought, struggled with, and always questioned. When rethinking higher education, it is necessary to rethink the learning system and campus environments to provide students different ways of knowing and to challenge their thinking to cultivate new paradigms and methods of discovery.[9]

THE FLEXIBLE EDUCATOR

The vast majority of educators teach because they are passionate about their subject and enjoy teaching and mentoring students. To stay current in their expertise, faculty engage in a continual process of professional development regarding content knowledge and their own pedagogical proficiency.

In addition, there is continuous learning of new technological innovations as well as refining and improving of instructional delivery of teaching and learning strategies so that faculty can continue to engage students in the content, assess learning, and be responsive to the college community they serve.[10]

Educators tend to be highly flexible professionals out of necessity or as a result of training.[11] During the COVID-19 pandemic, this flexibility was highly evident.

Moving seamlessly from a traditional classroom to fully online required a herculean change in teaching strategies and communication with students. Trying to effectuate this during an emergency pandemic yielded a variety of issues as it relates to faculty preparedness, student readiness, and university supports.[12]

As time away from the traditional classroom extended well beyond just a few weeks in spring 2020 and as campus buildings closed, virtual learning took center stage. Relying on educator flexibility and ingenuity, faculty reimagined their pedagogy and using existing technological resources of the institution, worked quickly to transition students to online instruction so as not to cause a break in learning.

Teaching is a human-facing profession that requires care and effort. For their own social and emotional support, faculty connected with other educators both inside and outside of their institutions using social media to exchange knowledge, garner personal or professional support, and build new skills.[13]

During the height of the pandemic, faculty were mindful of considering a whole student approach that included regular check-ins.[14] Each educator approached this differently with some utilizing one-on-one conferences, audio messages, restorative circles, or scheduled synchronous online meetings to help motivate students as well as continue the previously built classroom community.

Faculty became more flexible and students were given greater agency over their work in terms of due dates and alternative assignments. Good teaching adjusted to meet the needs of the current situation.

THE LEARNING EXPERIENCE

Learning is an intentional and experiential process. It is an active practice that results from a multiple step experience where the learner applies and deepens emerging skills. This experience can be intentional or unintentional, but either way there is a change in a behavior, performance, preferences, belief, or attitude.[15]

For maximum learning to take place in an educational environment, students must be engaged in experiences that require them to learn by doing and then have an opportunity to reflect on that experience. The opportunity to engage in hands-on learning through activities such as internships, practicums, study abroad, research, performances, clubs, sports activities, and activism is essential.

Unfortunately, during the COVID-19 pandemic, most of these activities were off limits to students and not available. To provide alternatives and substitutes, students were presented with real-world case studies and simulations. Videos and other forms of technology were utilized to deepen students' connection to their learning.[16] Active learning was used so students would be fully engaged in the learning process.

With the substitutions made, the intent was to keep students enthusiastically absorbed in their learning so that they could continue to pose questions, experiment, construct meaning, challenge decisions, and be accountable for their results.[17] Students were encouraged to push beyond facts and knowledge to think more critically about what was being learned to gain deeper intrinsic satisfaction about their work and to prevent disconnecting from the learning community.[18]

Throughout the transition to remote teaching, learning remained a social process. A variety of teaching and learning models were used throughout the pandemic to teach for both understanding and transfer of knowledge to other courses and the real world.[19] Two popular approaches used with the rapid transition to remote teaching—Universal Design for Learning (UDL) and Backward Design—are described below.

Universal Design for Learning

UDL focuses on learner needs and factors that influence learning and engagement. During remote teaching, the goal for many instructors was to find ways to create inclusive and flexible environments that would help lessen issues students were experiencing.

Accommodations included creating a curriculum that connected students to the *why*, *what*, and *how* of learning. Multiple means of action and expression were provided to allow students various ways to demonstrate their learning. UDL supports using meaningful ways to engage students by stimulating their interest in the material and information, so they dig deeper to make connections with the content and think about it in new ways.[20]

UDL activities help build fluency with the course content and highlight patterns, big ideas, and relationships to extend thinking. In addition, students can set their own learning goals and monitor their progress.

They collaborate in small groups and as a whole class to apply and practice what was learned. Assessments and reflections are used to gather information on acquired learning as well as to provide feedback.

UDL supports student learning by having students gather information, test their understanding, critique, and question new learning by working with others, creatively build on and present new ideas, and reflect on their process of learning.[21] Students are encouraged to take ownership of their learning even when they struggle.

Backward Design Model

A backward design means that instruction is planned with the end goals in mind. Learning goals are established before instructional methods and assessments are developed. Apart from building a community, a backward design refocuses instruction around specific learning outcomes rather than topics to be covered.

Backward design is a three-step process that starts with what is important for students to know about the content, then moves to what needs to be assessed to determine if the desired results were achieved and the standards met, and finishes with the instructional methods, strategies, and learning activities that will maximize student learning so that the students are equipped with the needed knowledge and skills and are able to demonstrate their understanding.[22]

TECHNOLOGY INTEGRATION

One major aspect of current teaching is the integration of technology. Various technologies can be used in the classroom to bring about more active forms of learning and fuller immersion into the content. Technology can complement a face-to-face classroom or be used to deliver fully online instruction.

Its use in almost all aspects of teaching and learning requires faculty to engage in professional development to explore various forms of interactive technologies and how they can be used in the classroom to share content as well as promote learning.

As technology usage increases across the campus and instructional modalities are improved, a strategic plan is useful for integrating these technologies effectively to include adequate faculty training and support services.[23] In addition, as more institutions provide course options that are more flexible, there is a continuing need for new investment in the technology itself.

Technology integration was at the heart of instruction throughout the COVID-19 pandemic using online learning and remote institutional services. Colleges and universities leveraged the use of technology by investing in new technologies and ensuring the use of course management systems for remote teaching and distance learning.

The CARES Act was a higher education relief fund passed by Congress in 2020 due to the pandemic. It provided emergency aid to colleges and helped purchase equipment such as conferencing software and computer hardware.[24]

Core technologies to support student success and retention were employed, such as online advising, early alerts, and degree progress tracking.[25] The top three technology-related skills requested most in faculty professional development during spring 2020 as colleges went remote included the following:

- video conferencing tools for group collaboration,
- posting digital materials online, and
- connecting virtually with students in need of social-emotional support.[26]

The need for high-speed internet and appropriate technologies is imperative in an online educational environment. Access to reliable internet remains a continuing challenge in the United States and abroad.

Until the infrastructure issues can be solved, utilizing fully online, synchronous aspects of virtual education cannot be fully realized. Issues of accessibility and infrastructure as they relate to equality and equity are considerable.

The pandemic showed us that students from higher socioeconomic backgrounds and certain geographic locations tended to have greater access to needed technologies due to where they lived or their socioeconomic status.[27]

Understandably, these students were able to connect more to their classes and subjects during remote instruction than those who did not have the technology resources or online access. Technology barriers and gaps in access persist in rural communities and among lower-income students, disproportionately impacting Black and Latinx students the most.[28]

MOVING FORWARD

This chapter focused on the transformational aspects of education. It explored teaching and learning as it was moved online at the start of the COVID-19 pandemic. It examined the instructional environment and the efforts made by faculty and staff to promote and support learning, as well as provide needed access to institutional services during this trying time.

The role of the faculty member as a passionate and caring professional was highlighted, as well as some of the barriers to learning experienced by students because of the pandemic. Emphasis was placed on building and supporting a community of learners so that students feel engaged and a part of the institution, even at a distance.

Best practices of teaching and learning were underscored that should serve as a continued focal point moving forward as it relates to intentional instructional design that reflects a learning environment adjusted and influenced based on student learning needs.

NOTES

1. "Policy Brief: Education during COVID-19 and Beyond," United Nations, August 2020, https://www.un.org/development/desa/dspd/wp-content/uploads/sites/22/2020/08/sg_policy_brief_covid-19_and_education_august_2020.pdf.

2. "Instructional Environment," National Center on Safe Supportive Learning Environments Office of Safe and Supportive Schools U.S. Department of Education, 2022, https://safesupportivelearning.ed.gov/topic-research/environment/instructional-environment.

3. John Hattie, *Visible Learning: A Synthesis of over 800 Meta-Analysis Relating to Achievement* (London: Routledge. 2009).

4. Richard H. Milner, *Start Where You Are, But Don't Stay There* (Harvard Education Press, 2020).

5. Viola Ardeni, Sara Dallavalle, and Karolina Serafin, "Building Student Communities in Spite of the COVID-19 Pandemic," *Journal of Teaching and Learning with Technology Special Issue* 10 (2021): 88–102.

6. "Framework for 21st Century Learning," Battelle for Kids, 2019, https://static.battelleforkids.org/documents/p21/P21_Framework_Brief.pdf.

7. Bri Stauffer, "What Are 21st Century Skills? Applied Educational Systems (AES)," January 19, 2022, https://www.aeseducation.com/blog/what-are-21st-century-skills.

8. Mary Deane Sorcinelli, "Research Findings on the Seven Principles," In *Applying the Seven Principles for Good Practice in Undergraduate Education* (New Directions for Teaching and Learning, no. 47. San Francisco: Jossey-Bass, 1991), 13–25.

9. Emma Sabzalieva, Eglis Chacón, Bosen Lily Liu, Diana Morales, Takudzwa Mutize, Huong Nguyen, and Jaime Roser Chinchilla, "Thinking Higher and Beyond: Perspectives on the Futures of Higher Education to 2050," United Nations Educational Scientific and Cultural Organization, 2021.

10. Lee Shulman, "Those Who Understand: Knowledge Growth in Teaching," *Educational Researcher* 12, no. 2 (1986): 4–14.

11. David A. Squires, William G. Huitt, and John K. Segars, "Improving Classrooms and Schools: What's Important," *Educational Leadership* 39, no. 3: (1981): 174–79.

12. Anya Kamanetz, "'Panic-gogy': Teaching Online Classes during the Coronavirus Pandemic," National Public Radio, March 2020, https://www.npr.org/2020/03/19/817885991/panic-gogy-teaching-online-classes-during-the-coronavirus-pandemic.

13. Torrey Trust, Jeffrey P. Carpenter, Daniel G. Krutka, and Royce Kimmons, "#RemoteTeaching & #RemoteLearning: Educator Tweeting during the COVID-19 Pandemic," *Journal of Technology and Teacher Education* 28. no. 2 (2020): 151–59.

14. Elizabeth Hehir, Marc Zeller, Joanna Luckhurst, and Tara Chandler, "Developing Student Connectedness under Remote Learning Using Digital Resources: A Systematic Review," *Education and Information Technologies* 26 (2021): 6531–48.

15. Marcy P. Driscoll and Kerry J. Burner, *Psychology of Learning for Instruction* (Hoboken, NJ: Pearson, 2022).

16. Michael Sankey, "Putting the Pedagogic Horse in Front of the Technology Cart," *Journal of Distance Education in China*, 5 (2020): 46–53.

17. David A. Kolb, *Experiential Learning: Experience as the Source of Learning and Development* (Upper Saddle River, New Jersey: Prentice Hall, [1984] 2014).

18. Mega B. Herlambang, Fokie Cnossen, and Niels A. Taatgen, "The Effects of Intrinsic Motivation on Mental Fatigue," *PLos One* 16, no. 1 (2021).

19. Julie Stern, Krista Ferraro, Kayla Duncan, Trevor Aleo, *Learning That Transfers: Designing Curriculum for a Changing World* (Thousand Oaks, CA: Corwin, 2021).

20. "The UDL Guidelines," CAST, 2022, https://udlguidelines.cast.org/.

21. George Siemens, "Learning and Knowing in Networks: Changing Roles for Educators and Designers," *FORUM for Discussion* (2008): 1–26.

22. Grant Wiggins and Jay McTighe, *Understanding by Design* (Alexandra, VA: Association for Supervision and Curriculum Development, 2005).

23. Beth McMurtrie, "The Coronavirus Has Pushed Courses Online. Professors Are Trying Hard to Keep Up," *The Chronicle of Higher Education,* March 20, 2020, https://www.chronicle.com/article/the-coronavirus-has-pushed-courses-online-professors-are-trying-hard-to-keep-up/.

24. "CARES Act," U.S. Department of Education Office of Postsecondary Education, https://www2.ed.gov/about/offices/list/ope/caresact.html.

25. Susan Grajek and D. Christopher Brooks, "How Technology Can Support Student Success during COVID-19," *Educause,* March 24, 2020, https://er.educause.edu/blogs/2020/3/how-technology-can-support-student-success-during-covid19.

26. Benjamin Herold, "How Tech-Driven Teaching Strategies Have Changed during the Pandemic," *Education Week,* April 14, 2022, https://www.edweek.org/technology/how-tech-driven-teaching-strategies-have-changed-during-the-pandemic/2022/04.

27. Alexsander Aristovnik, Damijana Kerzic, Dejan Ravselj, Nina Tomazevic, and Lan Umek, "Impacts of the COVID-19 Pandemic on Life of Higher Education Students: A Global Perspective," *Sustainability* 12, no. 20 (2020): 8438.

28. "Education in a Pandemic: The Disparate Impacts of COVID-19 on America's Students," Department of Education Office for Civil Rights, June 9, 2021, https://www2.ed.gov/about/offices/list/ocr/docs/20210608-impacts-of-covid19.pdf.

Chapter Three

Instructional Modalities

> *The most effective, successful professionals are constantly learning, they take the time to apply what they have learned, and they continually work to improve themselves.*
>
> —Joel Gardner

While the authenticity of face-to-face in-person instruction versus online instruction continues to be debated, the argument is becoming less focused on which modality is preferred for the student, the faculty member, or the institution, but rather on how students learn best.

This combined with the progression of online learning and its integration into almost all institutions of higher education in terms of a learning management system means that we are moving toward a hybrid model of face-to-face and online instruction. The extent to which each will be utilized is largely dependent on the institution or the individual faculty member.

Prior to the COVID-19 pandemic, approximately one third of higher education offered classes that were fully online.[1] When colleges and universities moved to remote learning in spring 2020, nearly every class was online.

Pre-pandemic research largely shows that students in online programs performed worse academically than students in face-to-face classes. On average, students taking online classes had lower grades, higher dropout rates, and poorer performance, and these outcomes were more prevalent for male students, students of color, and students with poor grades earlier in their education.[2]

What these earlier studies do not show, however, is how online teaching has improved over the years. There has been an increase in instructor engagement and online community building. Technology know-how and access has improved. And prior student demographics in terms of work issues and/or family concerns may have precipitated poorer outcomes as well as the unfamiliarity of teaching and learning at a distance.

In higher education today, courses are offered in a variety of modalities and times frames. Some are in the classroom and face-to-face spread over a full fifteen or sixteen weeks, offered during the fall or spring semester.

Others are fully online and virtual offered during this same traditional time frame or condensed into a seven- or eight-week accelerated course or even shorter time frame depending on whether it is a summer class or offered during "J" or January terms.

A popular option, as introduced earlier, is the hybrid format with a mixture of face-to-face and online learning. A newer modality, the hyflex model, was developed prior to the pandemic, but grew in popularity over the past several years because of the options it provides to students in terms of attendance and participation. In the hyflex model, students are given a choice in modality that works best for them for a given class.[3]

There is not a one-size-fits-all approach. Multiple factors come into play in terms of which teaching and learning option is most useful to a given student and which applies most pragmatically to a particular class or at a given point in the student's life.

The list is long and varied such as student age, motivation for learning, employment status, and family obligations. Some students benefit from instantaneous feedback in an in-person setting, some demand the flexibility of online learning, others prefer teamwork and collaboration, and for others accessibility is key.

Whatever forms of learning an institution of higher education adopts, the ability to evolve as student needs develop, as technology advances, and as the community progresses in terms of its industry, infrastructure capabilities, and culture are important in moving toward the most appropriate and useful instructional modalities.

Advancing the instructional environment amid change means providing students with the flexibility they need and the learning environment that suits them best. It means offering faculty options and training for teaching in different modalities with adequate resources and university support.

Successful integration of technology in higher education involves meeting the needs of both faculty and students in the instructional modality in which they are most comfortable while also successfully navigating information technology (IT) challenges within the institution itself.

Data and network security tops the list of IT challenges followed by student success support, IT staffing, data-enabled culture creation, digital integration, and data governance—and all are wrapped around the largest challenge for college IT departments—that of adapting to change.[4]

INSTRUCTIONAL MODALITIES

There are four primary modalities that largely dictate how faculty teach within higher education—in-person, online, hybrid, and hyflex.

In-person Instruction

Face-to-face or in-person instruction is the original method of teaching. An instructor is physically in the classroom with students in real time. The class is primarily lecture based though there may be group work within the classroom and other forms of discussion and engagement.

This type of modality has many benefits:

- Real-time interactions among faculty and students, as well as student-to-student contact in person
- Opportunities for instant engagement, simultaneous discussions, and immediate feedback
- Facilitation of in-person group work and other in-class opportunities for hands-on instruction

A face-to-face classroom has regular course meeting times that are on the college campus in a physical location. Students are expected to come to the in-person class prepared and having read the required readings ahead of time. Within the face-to-face class, there may be lecture, guest speakers, discussion, presentations, debate, group work, exams/quizzes, or other activities completed.

In-person learning has two distinct logistical drawbacks, namely that it is,

- limited in terms of a precise day/time for the class, and
- offered in one distinct physical location.

Today, most in-person learning in higher education is additionally supported by technology both within the classroom while the class is in real time as well as in a learning management system (LMS) or course management system (CMS).

Whether the LMS or CMS simply houses a course syllabus, accepts assignments, and/or administers exams—or the course housed in the LMS or CMS is more interactive in terms of discussions, group work, and resources—most current face-to-face classes include some form of technology or digital support.

Rare is the instructor in present day who hands out a paper syllabus, collects paper assignments, and gives scantron and paper exams with a #2 pencil.

Active learning strategies using technology integration can be added to the face-to-face class, such as online polls to check for understanding. These questions allow the faculty member to adjust the pace of the class based on student responses and understanding of the content, as well as facilitate further discussion based on new ideas and examples that may surface following the in-class polling exercise.[5]

Another strategy might be to offer "minute" papers at the end of a lesson or a class to reflect on what was just learned in the course with a follow-up question for clarification to indicate possible gaps in student knowledge.[6]

Small group work in the form of think-pair-share, role playing, peer review, and jigsaw class discussions are additional active learning opportunities that can be used in a face-to-face classroom to engage students, answer questions, and extend thinking about a topic.[7]

Online Learning

Online learning has been a lifeline in helping provide higher education to students who need flexibility when completing coursework. Also referred to as "distance" learning because it is the physical distance between the instructor and students during instruction.[8]

With online learning, students primarily use the internet to access the class and complete the requisite activities. The entire class is taught through an LMS or CMS that organizes materials and resources, activities and assessments, and communication and discussions.

The characteristics for online learning today are primarily the use of the internet using media, electronic texts, and programs for students and the instructor to interact with one another asynchronously—not in real time—throughout a learning module.

With the advancement of technology, institutions have been increasing the offerings of online and distance learning courses and programs. Given the extraordinary requirement during the pandemic, even more institutions are recognizing the value of moving classes online to meet the needs of students today.[9]

As more institutions provide fully online and/or hybrid course and program options, private-industry providers and other solutions such as course management producers and telecommunication companies will need to keep up with the demand.[10]

Asynchronous

In the asynchronous environment, students can participate in the course on days/times that are most convenient to them given parameters set-up by the instructor. The expectation is that certain readings, assignments, and assessments will be completed during a specified time period or "module." Modules may be set up in weeks to run from Monday through Sunday, for example, and students may be expected to post by a certain day/time during the module.

A learning module is logically structured and organized around collections of course content that focuses the student on a particular lesson or unit of study. It provides a pathway for the student to progress through the items within the module in an organized way, usually in sequential order.

Each module contains readings, multimedia, activities, discussions, and assessments, with options for adaptive release—pre-conditions set by the instructor—of activities or assessments. Each module must provide accessibility to all students from captions on images to closed captions per the Americans with Disabilities Act of 1990.[11]

Within an asynchronous online course, learners and the instructor interact at varying points during the module, such as multiple times weekly within the course. Students come-and-go throughout the week based on their own schedules and at times convenient to them.

In most online courses, there is peer-to-peer engagement coupled with instructor interaction, and this also tends to take place over time, rather than at the same time.[12] Students may choose to meet synchronously to work on a team project, for example, but in general most of their work is done remotely online.

The biggest advantages of online learning allow for the following:

- Flexible learning opportunities
- Geographical diversity of students and faculty
- Greater availability of programs and courses in time or place
- Response to student preferences for varied course delivery options

The prime benefit of asynchronous online learning is its adaptability. Many students are drawn to an online learning structure because their schedules and/or their physical location demands it.

Students in the military around the world, working parents, shift work, and people in varying parts of the globe or professions that are challenging either in terms of location or hours, need courses that are flexible with their professional responsibilities and personal constraints.

Opportunities for geographical diversity are a second strength. Students can interact with faculty and other students in an online class that come from around the world and in communities different than their own.

This opens up the class to greater levels of diversity in terms of thought and insight, which can help to broaden student mindsets and offer new ways of looking at problems and offering solutions.

Additionally, the fact that students themselves are not constrained by geographic or physical location means that a student can find a program of interest and enroll because of the credential, and/or courses offered, not because it is close to home.

This is helpful to both the institution in terms of attracting students nationally and even globally, and extremely useful to students in terms of providing opportunities for courses and programs that might not otherwise have been available to them if the classes were face-to-face or hybrid.

Many residential campuses that have traditionally focused on in-person classes are incorporating more online courses into their offerings post-pandemic to extend student choice. Colleges are using what they learned from remote teaching and providing students with course options and multiple modalities that students prefer.

Students are interested in various instructional modalities for their own flexibility and course scheduling. Now, they can experience the cohesiveness of an on-campus residential community with all the benefits of in-person classes and on-site campus activities, as well as take classes online and participate in virtual campus activities using technology. It truly is the best of both worlds for today's busy, multi-tasking college student.

There are also multiple drawbacks of online asynchronous learning. These include the following:

- Lonely and isolating
- Requirements for academic success are on the student
- Communication may "lag" because of the asynchronous nature
- Internet access is required

Learning online can be a lonely experience. While the class is fully online and there are multiple activities, assignments, and discussions for the students to complete, it is also just you and your computer. For students who require a lot of extrinsic motivation and need the consistent engagement with the instructor and other students in a real-time format, online asynchronous learning can feel very isolating and disconnected.

Fully online courses are also very individually driven. The student is ultimately the person responsible for being successful in the class. In a face-to-face class, the faculty member can motivate lower performing students to "step-up" and encourage students in ways that become more difficult online when the student and instructor cannot "see" each other in real time.

In a fully online class, the instructor is still "teaching," but the role is also one of a "facilitator" whereby the instructor helps the student with the material or assesses progress.

Also, in fully online classes, it is difficult for the instructor to know if the student is struggling unless the student reaches out, again because of this inability to fully "see" the student through the computerized classroom.

Rather than the instructor asking students how they are doing in a face-to-face class that meets at regular intervals in the classroom, in an online environment the student must initiate the conversation with the instructor or respond to the instructor when they reach out to the student. This is sometimes more difficult for introverted students, those who are struggling academically, or students from different cultures.

Some students also become frustrated with the asynchronous interactions because a discussion post made on Monday may take until Thursday to be responded to by a peer, for example.

Thus, it is difficult to tell who "hears" you in the fully online class because of the asynchronous aspect. The comment posted on Monday may not be read and responded to until many hours or days after the initial post and that delayed feedback can sometimes be lost or disconcerting for students.

And finally, access to the internet is required. The faster the better. Some colleges and universities have simple interfaces, and their online courses can be accessed easily by learners with lower technologies or slower internet service. Others require high speed internet access based on various course functions such as video, gaming, or other applications.

Synchronous

The other type of online learning is synchronous. This is where the online course shell exists with all the assignments and activities, but in addition to the online asynchronous components, there is also an online synchronous day/time when the class meets with the instructor via Zoom or another online interface.

Here the instructor conducts real-time instruction and engages with the students during a set day and time period. In a synchronous format there may be lecturing, as well as opportunities to ask real-time questions, hold discussions, and participate in small group activities.[13]

The synchronous component can be helpful to underscore important points made in the online course readings or to discuss concepts and theories and apply information in real time.

This type of synchronous online learning generally requires a strong internet connection, and therefore students or faculty with poor access or in remote locations will struggle with the synchronous component. Many students and faculty with internet insecurity experienced this during the pandemic.[14]

Online synchronous learning includes the following benefits:

- Real-time discussions
- Community can be developed more quickly and intimately due to the face-to-face interactions using technology
- Opportunities for small group interactions in "break-out" rooms
- Misconceptions or issues in learning and understanding can be dealt with quickly and questions can be immediately addressed

But there are drawbacks to online synchronous learning as well:

- Time zones matter, especially for international students
- Internet accessibility may be lacking for video and other high bandwidth course activities and some online platforms require huge data and high-speed access
- Zoom fatigue[15]

Whether asynchronous or synchronous, the use of technology during the pandemic produced higher adoption of digital tools and technology solutions that many faculty will continue using. This "forced exposure" of online learning during the pandemic resulted in many faculty and students finding online learning surprisingly palatable.

Hybrid or Blended Learning

A well-utilized form of learning is hybrid or blended learning. Hybrid learning is when learning is both online and asynchronous as well as face-to-face and synchronous. This form of teaching and learning attempts to combine the "best of both worlds" and gives students real-time access to the instructor and other students in the classroom environment as well as provides the flexibility of an online setting at alternate times.[16]

Blended learning extends the classroom environment and community beyond the walls of the traditional classroom.[17] Traditionally, the hybrid class in higher education has altered with a 50/50 split between online and face-to-face instruction—or 22.5 hours face-to-face and 22.5 hours of online activities in a typical class.

In a 3-credit course with the expectation of 45 contact hours (3 hours/week × 15 weeks of a traditional semester), students would attend class three hours per week face-to-face in a brick-and-mortar classroom at a designated time and place with the instructor and the other students. And then the second week of class would be fully online.

Another option would be to have students attend class face-to-face for approximately 1.5 hours and then complete the other 1.5 hours with online assignments during a given week.

Some schools have been creative with their approaches toward hybrid teaching and have varying amounts of online and face-to-face instruction.[18] This is popular during shorter terms, such as the "J" or January term where classes are highly accelerated and may only be two to three weeks in duration.

As an example, students may meet with their instructor and classmates in a synchronous in-person classroom at the beginning of the course. They then check in again in person mid-course, and then everyone meets up again in person at the end of the class.

Hybrid courses can be very beneficial to students because they offer the best of both worlds, for example, the instantaneous real-time interactions and the supportive community of a face-to-face class along with the flexibility of online learning.[19] Using a hybrid format can provide an improved level of performance and engagement because of the interactivity and flexibility that this format provides.[20]

As with other aspects of higher education, there is no one universal approach with regard to hybrid learning. Some students thrive in an online environment while others prefer face-to-face classes. While on the surface it seems ideal to simply put these two distinct student preferences together in a hybrid format, in reality it often does not work well for the affected student.

For students who have a distinct preference toward one instructional modality over the other, they may have difficulty adapting to the hybrid structure because of their learning preference or need for fully face-to-face instruction or a completely online classroom.

Deliberate actions and conversations must take place through academic advising when students are signing up for courses in different instructional modalities. The student must understand what the modality of "hybrid" means at a particular institution.

Faculty too may have divergent views, and this also needs to be discussed internally and an agreed-upon framework built whether it is in departments, colleges, or across campus so that students are clear on what a "hybrid" modality looks like at their institution.

Benefits of hybrid instruction include the following:

- Opportunity to combine face-to-face learning with online instruction
- Allows for some online flexibility
- Helpful for difficult topics that require 1:1 with an instructor in real time
- Useful for group work when everyone is in the classroom at the same time

Limitations of hybrid instruction include:

- Some students prefer—or truly need—online instruction and therefore may not be able to attend or engage in real-time face-to-face classes

- Some students prefer—or truly need—face-to-face instruction and therefore may not participate in the online portion of the course due to technology accessibility, insufficient knowledge about online learning, or lack of interest/motivation in completing course work online
- Class community suffers because both groups of students described above are not visible to their peers in the face-to-face class or participating in the course online

Hyflex

Hyflex learning is the newest instructional modality. It began as a blend of classroom and online instruction similar to the hybrid format, but within the hyflex model the instructor remains the focus of the course.[21] This modality has grown in popularity and interest.

Like hybrid instruction, hyflex is a combination of online learning and in-person instruction. It is both synchronous and asynchronous. The key difference is the level of flexibility this modality affords the student. Hyflex allows students to move back and forth between online and face-to-face learning depending on their preference or needs as the course progresses.

For illustration, take three students in a given class:

- One student attends the class face-to-face synchronously during the day/time it is held, as a traditional face-to-face class.
- A second student attends the class synchronously online from home through Zoom or another online platform provided.
- Due to scheduling conflicts or geographic limitations, the third student cannot attend online or in person in real time. Instead, this student views the class asynchronously online at another time convenient to the student.

All three students then participate together in an online activity within the course management system during the module asynchronously or synchronously if working together on a group project.

In hyflex, the level of flexibility provided to the instructor is less than that provided to the students. The instructor is committed to attending and leading the class at the day/time scheduled both with the students in the physical classroom as well as those attending virtually.

The instructor must also participate throughout the week or time period of a module online and asynchronously with the students in the class through the course management system. Synchronous office hours or meeting times are additionally set-up for students as needed.

Hyflex is centered around the following four principles:

1. Learner choice: Students choose how they want to attend each class throughout the course. Their choice can change from class-to-class depending on their own—not the instructor's—individual preferences or needs.
2. Equivalency: All activities should be designed so all groups—face-to-face or online and synchronous or asynchronous—can participate equally.
3. Reusability: Course content that is applicable to the face-to-face class should also be placed online and vice versa. Online content should be used by all members of the class regardless of the modality in which they enter the classroom.
4. Accessibility: Students have access to all parts of the class in equal measure whether in class, online, or participating asynchronously or synchronously. Every student has the same tools.[22]

While the hyflex modality promotes optimal equality and accessibility for all students in the course, the evolution of hyflex has meant different things to different instructors and within different educational institutions. Not everyone is as open to offering a class in as many different formats as possible at any given time. And not all students are successful in this modality even though it offers students multiple options and possibilities.

As with the hybrid modality, students need clear and accurate information prior to starting the class about what hyflex means to the institution. Students—especially those new to higher education—should be prepared and not just "dropped" into a hyflex class with little or no preliminary discussion or information about how the class works.

While the student may have a need for flexibility or want to be more independent in their learning, effective time management skills, good organizational skills, persistence, communication skills, reading and writing skills, level of motivation, and basic technical skills are all required components of a hyflex course.

An accepted definition of "engagement" needs to be discussed and agreed upon by both students and the faculty member teaching the class. Active learning strategies should be incorporated throughout the hyflex course whether in-person or online, and with both synchronous and asynchronous instruction.

Attendance and participation are both required in a hyflex course regardless of the modality the student selects. Even students with complicated personal and/or professional lives who perhaps might benefit most from the options offered through this modality must still take an active role in the hyflex classroom by completing activities and assignments by the due date and by maintaining contact with the instructor and participating with their classmates.

Here are the benefits of hyflex:

- Meets the needs of as many students as possible with regards to modalities and meeting times thereby allowing for more students to join the class who may have otherwise not been able to enroll.
- Has the potential to create various communities of learners.
- No matter which option students select for each class—online or face-to-face—they should be able to meet the same equivalent learning outcomes.
- Students can "try out" different modalities. For example, students who prefer in-person learning can try a synchronous online session or a fully asynchronous option.
- Convenient for students with improved access to learning.

Here are the drawbacks of hyflex:

- The instructor must be all things to all students, for example, in-person teacher and online facilitator.
- The instructor must be accessible both during the face-to-face class as well as throughout the week asynchronously to show an online presence.
- The instructor must be able to effectively balance teaching in multiple formats to meet the needs of the student and the curriculum.
- Students may be confused about the optionality offered with hyflex.
- Students may be "invisible" and not participate to the extent needed.
- Communities of learners may not interact to the degree needed to develop classroom community and learning opportunities.
- High speed internet access is mandatory for participating in the synchronous online sessions.

MOVING FORWARD

Throughout this chapter, learning options in various instructional modalities were discussed. As higher education transitioned into remote emergency teaching during the pandemic, it required faculty and students to work together to teach, communicate, and learn at a distance. The need for flexibility was intense and instantaneous.

As we approach a return to normal post-pandemic, there is a movement toward blended learning or a combination of face-to-face courses with more online learning options to provide flexibility for students, but still provide time and place connections, especially for traditional aged learners on residential campuses.

How to balance the needs of the campus environment with the advancement of technology to support learning in a manner that best meets the individual student needs as well as those of a changing society is the current challenge.

Ensuring that faculty, students, and the administration approach teaching and learning with an open mindset is important in terms of promoting flexibility and imagination in the learning process no matter under which modality a course is taught.

NOTES

1. Jon Marcus, "Momentum Builds behind a Three-Year Degree to Lower College Costs," *Washington Post*, April 2022, https://www.washingtonpost.com/education/2022/04/15/college-three-year-degree/.
2. Marcus, "Momentum Builds behind a Three-Year Degree to Lower College Costs."
3. Lucus Kohnke and Benjamin Luke Moorhouse, "Adopting HyFlex in Higher Education in Response to COVID-19: Students Perspectives," *The Journal of Open, Distance and eLearning* 36, no. 3. (2021): 231–44.
4. Stephen Sweett, "7 Technology and IT Challenges in Higher Education," University Business, December 17, 2020, https://universitybusiness.com/7-technology-and-it-challenges-in-higher-education/.
5. John Rich, "Polling Students to Check Understanding," Edutopia, December 14, 2017, https://www.edutopia.org/article/polling-students-check-understanding/.
6. Thomas P. Angelo and K. Patricia Cross, *Classroom Assessment Techniques: A Handbook for College Teachers* (San Francisco: Jossey-Bass,1993): 148–53.
7. Elizabeth F. Barkley and Claire Howell Major, *Engaged Teaching: A Handbook for College Faculty* (The K. Patricia Cross Academy, 2022).
8. Joi L. Moore, Camille Dickson-Deane, and Krista Galyen, "eLearning, Online Learning, and Distance Learning Environments: Are they the Same?" *The Internet of Higher Education* 14, no. 2 (2011): 129–35.
9. Marko Teräs, Juha Suoranta, Hanna Teräs, and Mark Curcher, "Post-COVID-19 Education and Education Technology 'Solutionism': A Seller's Market," *Postdigital Science and Education* 2 (2020): 863–78.
10. Nadine Diaz-Infante, Michael Lazar, Samvitha Ram, and Austin Ray, "Demand for Online Education Is Growing. Are Providers Ready?" McKinsey & Company, 2023, https://www.mckinsey.com/industries/education/our-insights/demand-for-online-education-is-growing-are-providers-ready.
11. "Auxiliary Aids and Services for Postsecondary Students with Disabilities," U.S. Department of Education, https://www2.ed.gov/about/offices/list/ocr/docs/auxaids.html.
12. DLINQ Staff Contributors, *The Asynchronous Cookbook* (Self-Publis. Open Textbook Library, 2021).
13. Nada Dabbagh, Rose M. Marra, and Jane L. Howland, *Meaningful Online Learning: Integrating Strategies, Activities, and Learning Technologies for Effective Designs* (London: Routledge, 2018).
14. "Education in a Pandemic: The Disparate Impacts of COVID-19 on America's Students," U.S. Department of Education Office for Civil Rights, June 9, 2021, https://www2.ed.gov/about/offices/list/ocr/docs/20210608-impacts-of-covid19.pdf.

15. DLINQ Staff Contributors, *The Asynchronous Cookbook*, 2021.

16. Joi L. Moore et al., "eLearning, Online Learning, and Distance Learning Environments."

17. Barbara Means, Yukie Toyama, Robert Murphy, and Marianne Baki, "The Effectiveness of Online and Blended Learning: A Meta-Analysis of the Empirical Literature," *Teachers College Record* 115, no. 3 (2013): 1–47.

18. D. Randy Garrison and Norman D. Vaughan, *Blended Learning in Higher Education: Framework, Principles, and Guidelines* (San Francisco, CA: Wiley Jossey-Bass, 2012).

19. Keely Steele and Lovely Singh, "Combining the Best of Online and Face-to-Face Learning: Hybrid and Blended Learning Approach for COVID-19, Post Vaccine, and Post-Pandemic World," *Journal of Educational Technology Systems* 50. no. 2. (2021): 140–71.

20. Anthony Francescucci and Mary Foster, "The VIRI (Virtual, Interactive, Real-Time, Instructor-Led) Classroom: The Impact of Blended Synchronous Online Courses on Student Performance, Engagement, and Satisfaction," *Canadian Journal of Higher Education* 43, no. 3 (2013): 78–91.

21. Wenliang He, Daniel Gajski, George Farkas, and Mark Warschauer, "Implementing Flexible Hybrid Instruction in an Electrical Engineering Course: The Best of Three Worlds?" *Computers & Education 81* (2015): 59–68.

22. Brian J. Beatty, *Hybrid-Flexible Course Design* (EdTech Books, 2019), https://edtechbooks.org/hyflex.

Chapter Four

Transforming Opportunities for Learning

Once you have learned to ask questions—relevant and appropriate and substantial questions—you have learned how to learn and no one can keep you from learning whatever you need to know.

—Neil Postman and Charles Weingartner,
Teaching as a Subversive Activity

The world into which students are entering is changing and so are their opportunities for learning. Personal branding and responsibility for one's own career is now more the norm than an exception.

No longer do graduating seniors expect to be at an organization for an entire career. Nor will they accept the same 8 a.m. to 5 p.m., Monday through Friday routine of the baby boom generation.

What students want from an employer is shifting, and what employers can give has evolved. Technologies continue to advance resulting in multifaceted careers that require varying knowledge and skills predicated on these new advancements.

What does this mean for higher education? For starters, it means that the social contract upon which students enter the community of higher education is fluid in terms of goals. Common values include fairness, respect, care, and honesty.[1] These values should continue unabated in classrooms and community spaces throughout the campus.[2]

As discussed later in this book, the forward movement of higher education will be in keeping with the ideals of a learning organization. An organization that can learn while growing and advancing technological and educational opportunities for faculty and students, while also preparing students for the knowledge economy post-graduation.[3]

The global economy is constantly shifting in various cycles from recession to expansion and back again based on various macroeconomic conditions like employment, prices, interest rates, and inflation.[4] International needs for labor are changing, and there are technology advancements that require adjustment or reeducation for the current worker.

Goals in terms of what each student is looking for are changing as learners evolve in terms of who they are becoming both professionally and personally. Beyond the Great Resignation, we are now amid the Great Reshuffle with employees seeking better work–life balance and control over their time and working conditions.[5]

Higher education must continue to reinvent itself to meet the social and economic challenges of today. This includes the current Gen Z traditional-aged student as well as the retraining of the knowledge-worker where there is a continuous upskilling and reskilling of expertise and credentials.

This new knowledge and retooling of skills that students demand while learning to use new and emerging technologies must be offered in a scaffolded manner that yields continuous improvement and sequential advancement to students throughout their careers and entrepreneurial endeavors.

While traditional two-year and four-year degree programs, as well as graduate education, will continue to be part of colleges and universities worldwide, additional timely, pragmatic, and innovative educational options must be added to respective curriculums to assist in developing the advanced instruction students need for today and tomorrow.[6]

CURRENT ISSUES

There has been a collective focus on students who enroll in college but do not graduate. According to the National Center for Education Statistics, roughly three out of five students who enroll in college complete a degree or certificate program within six years.[7] Some 36 million people in the United States have earned some college credit but not an actual degree.[8]

Lack of financial resources has been a major impediment with students not realizing that financial aid was available. In addition, some find the transfer process from a two-year college to a four-year university so complicated that some students give up. And for others, requirements like math are obstacles that continue to challenge students' ability to complete a college degree and graduate.[9]

The continued enhancements in program and degree offerings, to include cross-institutional partnerships, incorporating new and emerging technologies, use of online instructional models, and other creative endeavors to meet new challenges and provide opportunities to innovate higher education are currently being undertaken.

Colleges are using institutional data to capture information on demographic trends, learning behaviors, and costs of instruction and instructional support to ensure these transformations are meeting students current and future needs.[10]

What follows is a sampling of present-day opportunities and additions being offered in a variety of college curriculums to attract students, improve retention, and ensure completion of courses, programs, and ultimately degrees.

TRANSFORMATIVE INITIATIVES

These initiatives can be life-changing for the student, helpful to the institution, and supportive of the community at large in terms of advancing the economy and improving the overall well-being of its citizens with workforce development.[11]

The nation's community colleges and technical institutions have been at the forefront of highly impactful initiatives in higher education.[12] Many have updated mission statements to reaffirm their support given the pandemic crisis and are working to build a culture of equity and advancement of social justice through education.[13]

Classes are offered in a variety of modalities and students can select the format most appropriate to their learning needs and personal circumstances. While trying to limit tuition and fee increases, colleges have also been working diligently to reduce costs for textbooks and other supplies.[14]

The pandemic brought a surge in demand for food and other basic necessities mitigated successfully through food pantries on campus as well as partnerships with community agencies to help students with housing insecurities.[15]

Post-pandemic, what students want out of a college experience is changing. When students come to college, for example, some wish to "go slow" while others need an accelerated completion. On residential campuses, many full-time students are deciding not to live on campus.[16]

In light of these social, economic, and technological changes, many institutions are offering credits and courses in new and transformative ways, both through distance learning and on-campus, to provide value and future usefulness for students.[17]

Being a nimble institution and incorporating agility and flexibility into the college experience in terms of options and support for the student is imperative.[18] Some of the most popular initiatives are discussed below.

Stackable Credentials

Students can earn certificates and degrees in a "stackable" format. Each prior credential builds on the other and can provide incremental milestones toward a culminating degree. Many of the certificates and degree programs are aligned with specific industry requirements to ensure value in the labor market.[19]

Combining stackable credentials with credits for prior learning or work experience, military service, or other education such as Peace Corps service can increase access to postsecondary education and allow students to receive credit for competencies mastered prior to—or even concurrently—while attending college.

It can also allow for easy exit from the educational institution if the workplace credential earned serves a purpose at a certain point, and then provide a seamless on-ramp for down the road should the student want to reengage in pursuit of a second credential, course, or degree.[20]

This highway metaphor allows students to pursue credentialing when it makes sense to do so and with the appropriate recognition of prior learning, as well as ensures that students can come and go from taking courses as needed throughout their careers.

There are multiple benefits to implementing stackable credentials both for the institution, the community, and the students themselves. These include opportunities to build long-term partnerships with business and industry in local communities and geographic regions to identify current and future workforce needs.[21]

Students are better prepared for in-demand employment opportunities because local industry representatives have validated the job skills needed at the present time for the workplace. They ensure that a program's instruction and work-based learning experiences are on par with what is needed in the workplace.[22]

Often representatives from these organizations sit on program advisory boards and are active in recommending courses and programmatic needs based on industry direction. This is especially helpful in programs that have a high employee demand, such as nursing, hospitality, or engineering.

In addition, for many in-demand occupations such as cybersecurity, industry certifications are standard practice. Colleges can embed specific certifications within programs to provide students with needed credentials that are required by employers and go beyond the programmatic credential.

Stackable credentials provide students with the skills they need in a "just-in-time" manner. Career pathways are set up to include multiple entry and exit points for obtaining different credentials offered by the institution with a clear through-line to the culminating degree.

Attention must be paid to course delivery options to ensure that classes are offered when and how students most need them. Being flexible and responsive to all students is a challenge, especially as basic needs of students increase such as housing, childcare, or food.[23]

The use of stackable credentials is one approach to providing more varied opportunities for obtaining educational credentials. According to the U.S. Department of Education, stackable credentials:

- provide students with needed flexibility in taking courses and completing certificates or degrees,
- meet employer needs by assuring needed skills are provided through higher education, and
- allow educational institutions to improve outcomes for student achievement of postsecondary credentials, which is especially important among underserved populations.[24]

Scaffolding the learning process through stackable credentials is an innovative approach to promote singular opportunities that bind together into one culminating degree.[25] Students can achieve career advancement with short term rewards and at the same time accrue longer-term gains toward associate, baccalaureate, and/or advanced degrees.[26]

Business Partnerships

Business partnerships within higher education have also generated considerable attention, especially among popular technology companies like Amazon, Google, Apple, and Microsoft.[27] Community colleges are often prime recipients for public-private partnerships. Traditionally these collaborations have centered around career and workforce development programs.

Recent partnerships focused on worker shortages and in-demand positions:

- Amazon invested in a pilot program in Washington state to address the computer science shortage by building on the national trend of community college's offering bachelor's degrees.[28] This offers a win-win to community colleges trying to address the "skills gap," giving students opportunities to be successful within in-demand fields and providing qualified employees to Amazon and other companies constrained by worker shortages.
- Google has focused on increasing access to underrepresented groups through their "Grow with Google" digital skills training program. The company recently announced expansion of their Google Career Certificate program that will further community college as well as four-year university partnerships to help prepare students for in-demand jobs by turning the Google Career Certificates into college credit.[29]
- Microsoft announced a national campaign to work with U.S. community colleges to expand the cybersecurity workforce both in number and diversity.[30]

Their support extends beyond student scholarships to faculty training, as well as tools and administrative capacity, with plans to work with four-year colleges as well.[31]

Institutional Partnerships

Also critical is building partnerships not just with local industry but with other higher educational institutions as well. School partnerships are on the rise, whether between institutions or with industry.[32] A technical school with a strong engineering or mathematics focus for example, may find it beneficial to partner with another institution known for its liberal arts expertise.[33]

The nation's community and technical colleges are critical access points for first-generation college students.[34] Ensuring that they offer various forms of degree programs and continuing professional development with certifications, internships, and apprenticeship opportunities that can be carried forward is essential.

Guaranteeing and improving transferability of courses, certificates, and programs can help students advance into higher level degrees and build on their knowledge—and credentials—when ready.

Guaranteed and Dual Admissions

In this innovative arrangement, students are accepted to both a two-year community college and a four-year college or university at the same time. This partnership between the two institutions has the propensity to benefit students as they work toward a bachelor's degree.

Most students who enroll in a community college are interested in the bachelor's degree, yet less than 10 percent of students in a six-year follow-up study have done so.[35]

These guaranteed transfer opportunities are increasing across campuses, most between in-state schools with some out-of-state guaranteed admissions pacts as well. Students are in contact with the four-year university advisor while still enrolled in their first two years at the community college. With this dual-admissions guarantee, students are acclimated to the culture of both institutions at the same time.

Some universities offer scholarships to students who maintain certain grade point averages and students have the reassurance that the credits completed at the community college will transfer to the four-year institution.

Institutional Course Sharing

Some institutions are seeing benefits of sharing faculty and/or courses across institutions. This is especially popular in courses or programs that have experienced declining enrollments or when trying to offer students access to a greater range of courses, such as foreign language instruction.[36]

For colleges needing to conserve funds or for those simply wanting to provide additional options to their students, this can ensure students have access to instruction that otherwise may not have been open to them at their current institution.[37]

Micro-credentials

Based on students and industries changing needs in the evolution of education, micro-credentials are gaining in popularity. Intent on closing the "skills gap" to provide qualified candidates to satisfy available jobs, the National Education Association defines a micro-credential as a short, competency-based recognition that can be personalized, flexible, and performance-based with demonstrated mastery of the subject matter.[38]

Also called "badges," micro-credentials are super-focused and align with skills most needed by employers. Micro-credentials help students master in-demand skills in shorter learning time than a formal degree and provide flexible opportunities to gain skills and competencies to add a new skill, advance in a career, or round out a degree program.

These shorter-term opportunities allow students to transition to or within careers in less time and at a lower cost than a more formal degree program. Micro-credentials tend to be adaptable with flexible start dates when students are ready to reskill, upskill, or receive credentialing to enter a new field or improve upon an existing vocation.

Credit for Prior Learning

Credit for prior learning, also known as prior learning assessment, has been around for some time in higher education. It is once again gaining interest as colleges and universities look to provide the best possible opportunities to their students. It is often overlooked as a useful strategy for helping adult learners earn college credit for their accumulated expertise.

Credit for prior learning translates a student's prior work and life experience into college credits. Skills a student gained outside the classroom from work, military service, travel, hobbies, civic activities, and volunteer service are evaluated to award credit that can be applied toward a certificate or degree program.

Multiple methods may be used to assess prior learning. These can include student portfolios of past work and/or experiences or standardized exams to verify knowledge such as the College Level Examination Program (CLEP) or the DANTES Subject Standardized Tests.[39]

The American Council on Education (ACE) publishes "Learning Evaluations" for nontraditional training completed outside traditional degree programs. For example, in collaboration with the Department of Defense, ACE reviews a student's military training and experiences so college credit can be received.[40]

Credit for prior learning can reduce the number of classes needed for a degree given previous experience and prior knowledge. Having prior learning assessed may provide the "bridge" for some students and reduce their time until graduation. This ultimately makes education more affordable and results in less time toward program completion, which can help with student persistence and retention.

Apprenticeship Programs

Multiple states are offering new teacher apprenticeship programs that help develop K-12 teacher pipelines. Tennessee is one of several states approved by the U.S. Department of Labor to offer a "Grow Your Own" initiative to develop K–12 teachers and provide teacher licensure post-pandemic when national teacher shortages are at an all-time high.[41] The program offers a no-cost pathway into the teaching profession with programmatic supports such as tutoring and coaching.[42]

The apprenticeship program serves three different types of students:

- those in a career or technical program in high school;
- current school staff, such as paraprofessionals, who do not currently hold an undergraduate degree; and
- those transitioning to a new career who already hold a bachelor's degree but no teaching credential or master's degree.[43]

This fully funded learn-while-you-earn workforce development model gives colleges direct access to potential teachers from a variety of sources in the community. Universities are quickly jumping on board from across the country to offer their support for this K–12 teacher apprenticeship initiative.

Tennessee is just one of many states responding to the call to action from the U.S. Department of Education with recent announcements also made in California, New Mexico, Delaware, and Iowa.[44]

By industry, apprenticeships are occurring most notably in construction, public administration, and educational services. As of 2021, there were over twenty-five thousand active apprenticeship programs available with over half a million people actively enrolled in a nationally registered apprenticeship program.[45]

Accelerate Time to Completion

The pandemic has created a sense of urgency and today's students are impatient to see academic progression or need fast-paced career transitions. Faster, cheaper, and with convenience is the new norm. These are not terms typically attributed to higher education.

NewU University, a private nonprofit degree granting educational institution, is licensed to issue a three-year on-campus bachelor's degree at a lower tuition price point than other private nonprofit institutions. They have also promised not to raise tuition for the three years it will take a student to earn a bachelor's degree.[46]

Opening in fall 2023, NewU's approach is to lengthen traditional fifteen-week semesters to eighteen weeks and increase course credits from three to four to reach the traditional 120 credits required for the undergraduate degree.[47]

Other colleges and universities nationwide are also looking at three-year degrees for some majors. Called "College in 3," this trend had not gained a lot of traction over the past decade, but that could change as we emerge from the pandemic with more people interested in nontraditional approaches to obtaining a degree at a lower cost.[48]

Traditionally, three-year degrees meant a student had to add summer sessions and/or take additional classes beyond a full credit load. Social opportunities could be diminished for the traditional-aged student as well, such as participating in clubs, sports, and other campus events given the accelerated three-year time frame.

While some students may be highly motivated with this model, the pace may be too accelerated for others. Most recently, some schools are experimenting with ways to offer a three-year degree program that still allows for summer breaks, holidays, and an on-campus experience.

There are hurdles, such as total credit hours needed for graduation as well as accreditation requirements. But as schools consider new approaches for adult, nontraditional, and career-focused students, this could be a worthwhile solution.[49] Especially when cost, time, and access are issues.

Another popular option for some universities has been to combine a bachelor's degree with a master's degree in the four years it takes to traditionally complete the bachelor's degree. It is called a 4+1 program, where students in their senior year of their undergraduate program begin working on their graduate degree.[50]

Dual Enrollment

Community college and high school partnerships have been a successful option to helping students seamlessly transition into colleges and universities.

Dual enrollment among high school students has been one reason community colleges have roared back post-pandemic in terms of enrollments by over 10 percent in 2022.[51]

During the COVID-19 pandemic, many colleges stopped using placement testing for high school students. As a result, more high school students began participating in dual enrollment programs.

As we move from the pandemic, the utility of placement test scores to assign incoming students to either developmental or college-level courses in math and English is being questioned with preference for using multiple assessment measures to evaluate students prior to placement.[52]

Research has shown that there are racial and ethnic gaps in dual enrollment participation. African American and Hispanic students who have greater income disparity are less likely to participate in dual enrollment programs, primarily because they lack access to advanced placement courses or entrance testing keeps them from participating.[53] More critical evaluation is needed to ensure equity and equal opportunity with dual enrollment for all students.

For students who do participate in dual enrollment, studies have found that it has a positive effect on high school graduation rates, college enrollment and grades, and eventual completion of a college degree.[54]

When colleges and high school partners work together to create equitable placement policies that use multiple measures of assessment, along with policies that provide academic, financial, and social support for students, more students can benefit from dual enrollment programs with colleges serving as the passageway for program completion and prepared graduates.[55]

Utilizing dual enrollment can offer higher education to traditionally underserved students and promote socioeconomic mobility.[56] By taking college classes while still in high school, students are able to gain greater confidence in their academic abilities to succeed at college-level work.

A major challenge for colleges with popular dual enrollment options has been in having enough faculty to support the dually enrolled student as well as students enrolled in other college courses throughout the institution.

Creative solutions must be investigated for finding qualified faculty. These could include the following:

- utilizing high school teachers as college adjuncts with support from faculty liaisons,
- having college professors go into secondary schools or high school students coming directly onto the college campus,
- searching out opportunities to partner with local graduate programs to have students there teach dually enrolled students as part of their graduate degree program, and

- providing tuition assistance or reimbursement to high school teachers who hold a master's degree but lack the required eighteen graduate credit hours in the content area to teach dually enrolled students.[57]

The addition of dual enrollment programs has been helpful to high school students as well as the community colleges themselves as they transition away from the pandemic and toward a brighter future. High school students benefit from these pathways, especially when states and institutions create equitable policies that positively advance dual enrollment opportunities.[58]

MOVING FORWARD

Higher education is expanding new opportunities for students in getting what they want out of their educative process. Whether this is a single course, micro-credential, dual enrollment, or a college degree. Institutions are working together to provide college partnerships that benefit the student and improve the institution's own opportunities and sustainability.

Thus, whether higher education is supporting the high school student through dual enrollment, the returning military veteran through credit for prior learning, or adult learners interested in reskilling or upskilling, or any number of other potential students, there are opportunities for students and for higher education going forward.

We are seeing renewed energy and focus from federal and state governments to support students in their learning and to help open doors through revised student loan programs, grants, and other possibilities. In addition, the impact of private industry on education cannot be understated. Working hand in glove with industry, these partnerships will help support education as it moves forward and meets student needs in purposeful and timely ways.

Higher education is listening to industry demands and trying to find innovative ways to work with businesses and government in unity toward training students for the jobs of the future and providing qualified and talented employees to the local community in support of the national economy.

It is incumbent upon educational institutions to help students "finish what they start" by emphasizing strong student support, not just in the classroom but also throughout their educational journey, with a variety of services in student advising, financial aid, career planning, and others.[59]

As higher education plans for its future post-pandemic and adjusts to changing needs and demands of its constituents, investigating these—and future—opportunities more deeply will only increase. Continuing to find avenues for opening up access to students in more equitable ways will also accelerate and advance future possibilities.

NOTES

1. Doris Schroeder, Kate Chatfield, Michelle Singh, Roger Chennells, and Peter Heissone-Kelly, "The Four Values Framework: Fairness, Respect, Care and Honesty," in *Equitable Research Partnerships* (Springer, Cham. 2019).

2. Richard L. Curwin, "Create a Partnership with Your Students When Designing Your Social Contract," *ASCD*, April 25, 2014, https://www.ascd.org/blogs/create-a-partnership-with-your-students-when-designing-your-social-contract.

3. Zachary Simpson, "Reimagining Higher Education in the Wake of COVID-19," *Scholarship of Teaching and Learning in the South* 4, no. 1 (2020): 1–3.

4. Eshe Nelson and Melissa Eddy, "European Central Bank Raises Rates Again as Eurozone Inflation Persists," *The New York Times*, February 2, 2023, https://www.nytimes.com/2023/02/02/business/european-central-bank-interest-rates.html.

5. Paddy Hirsch, "How the Pandemic Changed the Rules of Personal Finance," National Public Radio, January 31, 2023, https://www.npr.org/sections/money/2023/01/31/1152162432/how-the-pandemic-changed-the-rules-of-personal-finance.

6. "Innovating Education and Educating for Innovation: The Power of Digital Technologies and Skills," OECD Center for Educational Research and Innovation, 2016, https://www.oecd.org/education/ceri/GEIS2016-Background-document.pdf.

7. "Undergraduate Retention and Graduation Rates Condition of Education," U.S. Department of Education Institute of Education Sciences National Center for Education Statistics, 2022, https://nces.ed.gov/programs/coe/indicator/ctr.

8. Rebecca Koenig, "Mapping Out a 'Credential as You Go' Movement for Higher Education," EdSurge, May 4, 2021, https://www.edsurge.com/news/2021-05-04-mapping-out-a-credential-as-you-go-movement-for-higher-education.

9. Jill Barshay, "Why So Few Students Transfer from Community Colleges to Four-Year Universities," The Hechinger Report, June 2020, https://hechingerreport.org/why-so-few-students-transfer-from-commun.

10. Christian Fischer, Zachary A. Pardos, Ryan Shaun Baker, Joseph Jay Williams, Padraic Smyth, Renzhe Yu, Stefan Slater, Rachel Baker, and Marc Warschauer, "Mining Big Data in Education: Affordances and Challenges," *Review of Research in Education* 44, no. 1 (2020): 130–60.

11. Richard Arum and Mitchell L. Stevens, "Building Tomorrow's Workforce Today: Twin Proposals for the Future of Learning, Opportunity, and Work," Hamilton Project, 2020, https://www.hamiltonproject.org/assets/files/PP_ArumStevens_LO_FINAL.pdf.

12. Bernard A. Polnariev and Mitchell A. Levy, "#SocialEquityMatters: A Multimodal Approach to Strengthening Student Success Through Innovation," in *Bridging Marginality through Inclusive Higher Education: Neighborhoods, Communities, and Urban Marginality* (Palgrave Macmillan, Singapore, 2022), 203–33.

13. "American Association of Community Colleges Puts Spotlight on CSM's Mission, COVID-19 Response," College of Southern Maryland, December 3, 2020, https://www.csmd.edu/news/2020/12/american-association-of-community-colleges-puts-spotlight-on-csms-mission,-covid-19-response.html.

14. Farran Powell, Emma Kerr, and Josh Moody, "12 Ways to Cut Your Textbook Costs," *U.S. News & World Report*, August 17, 2021, https://www.usnews.com/education/best-colleges/paying-for-college/slideshows/ways-to-cut-your-textbook-costs.

15. Madeline St. Amour, "Greater Need for Food at Community Colleges," Inside Higher Ed, January 7, 2021, https://www.insidehighered.com/news/2021/01/07/community-colleges-see-demand-food-bank-services-swell.

16. "Trends in College Pricing 2018," College Board Trends in Higher Education Series, 2018, https://research.collegeboard.org/media/pdf/trends-college-pricing-2018-full-report.pdf.

17. "Digest of Education Statistics," Table 311.15, "Number and Percentage of Students Enrolled in Degree-Granting Postsecondary Institutions, by Distance Education Participation, Location of Student, Level of Enrollment, and Control and Level of Institution: Fall 2017 and Fall 2018," National Center for Education Statistics Institute of Education Sciences, 2020, Washington, DC.

18. Richard P. Keeling, "Learning Reconsidered: A Campus-Wide Focus on the Student Experience," National Association of Student Personnel Administrators and American College Personnel Association, 2004, https://www.utep.edu/student-affairs/_Files/docs/Assessment/Learning-Reconsidered.pdf.

19. Katharine E. Meyer, Kelli A. Bird, and Benjamin L. Castleman, "Stacking the Deck for Employment Success: Labor Market Returns to Stackable Credentials" (EdWorkingPaper, Annenberg Institute at Brown University, 2022), 20–317.

20. Rory McGreal and Don Olcott, "A Strategic Reset: Micro-Credentials for Higher Education Leaders," *Smart Learning Environments* 9, no. 9 (2022).

21. Rory McGreal and Don Olcott, "A Strategic Reset."

22. Geoffrey M Cox, *Theorizing the Resilience of American Higher Education: How Colleges and Universities Adapt to Changing Social and Economic Conditions* (London, UK: Routledge, 2020).

23. "#Realcollege 2021: Basic Needs Insecurity during the Ongoing Pandemic," The Hope Center, March 31, 2021, https://hope.temple.edu/sites/hope/files/media/document/HopeNationalReport2021-22-compressed-compressed.pdf.

24. "Mapping Upward: Stackable Credentials That Lead to Careers," Perkins Collaborative Resource Network, December 2022, https://cte.ed.gov/initiatives/community-college-stackable-credentials.

25. Paul Freedman and Paul LeBlanc, "Let's Make This the 'Year of Stackability,'" Inside Higher Ed, June 11, 2021, https://www.insidehighered.com/views/2021/06/11/credentials-must-be-stackable-if-were-educate-adult-learners-successfully-opinion.

26. Ray Schroeder, "Higher Ed Curricula—The Short Game," Inside Higher Ed, October 2022, https://www.insidehighered.com/digital-learning/blogs/online-trending-now/higher-ed-curricula%E2%80%94-short-game.

27. Ryan M. Cameron, "Why High-Tech and Education Partnerships Work," LinkedIn, October 1, 2019, https://www.linkedin.com/pulse/why-high-tech-higher-education-partnerships-work-ryan-m-cameron.

28. Dean Golembeski, "Amazon Invests in Community College Bachelor's Degree Programs," Best Colleges, January 24, 2022, https://www.bestcolleges.com/news/2022/01/24/amazon-washington-community-colleges-computer-science/.

29. Ruth Porat, "Expanding Pathways into Higher Education and the Workforce," Google [blog], October 29, 2021, https://blog.google/outreach-initiatives/grow-with-google/higher-education-partnerships/.

30. Mark J. Drozdowski, "Google, Microsoft Promote Tech Careers through Community Colleges," Best Colleges, May 6, 2022, https://www.bestcolleges.com/news/analysis/2021/11/15/google-microsoft-tech-careers-community-colleges/.

31. Brad Smith, "America Faces a Cybersecurity Skills Crisis: Microsoft Launches National Campaign to Help Community Colleges Expand the Cybersecurity Workforce," Microsoft [blog], October 28, 2021, https://blogs.microsoft.com/blog/2021/10/28/america-faces-a-cybersecurity-skills-crisis-microsoft-launches-national-campaign-to-help-community-colleges-expand-the-cybersecurity-workforce/.

32. "Bachelors to Graduate Degree Accelerated Programs," University of Mary Washington Partner Programs, January 21, 2023, https://cas.umw.edu/beyond/partnership-programs/.

33. Judith Crown, "Confronting the Cliff: A Declining School-Age Population Leaves Small Colleges at a Crossroads," *Crain's Chicago Business*, August 26, 2022, https://www.chicagobusiness.com/crains-forum-higher-education/colleges-universities-student-population-enrollment-cliff.

34. Melinda Mechur Karp, Maria Cormier, Sarah E. Whitley, Sarah M. Umbarger-Wells, and Alexis Wesaw, "First-Generation Students in Community and Technical Colleges: A National Exploration of Institutional Support Practices," Center for First-Generation Student Success NASPA–Student Affairs Administrators in Higher Education Phase Two Advisory, 2020, https://firstgen.naspa.org/research-and-policy/community-and-technical-college-report.

35. Jon Marcus, "A New Way to Help College Students Transfer: Admit Them to Two Schools at Once," The Hechinger Report, June 29, 2022, https://hechingerreport.org/a-new-way-to-help-college-students-transfer-admit-them-to-two-schools-at-once/.

36. Crown, "Confronting the Cliff."

37. Schroeder, "Higher Ed Curricula."

38. "Micro-Credentials," National Education Association, 2022, https://www.nea.org/professional-excellence/professional-learning/micro-credentials.

39. Rebecca Klein-Collins, "Fueling the Race to Postsecondary Success," The Council for Adult and Experiential Learning (CAEL), March 2010, https://files.eric.ed.gov/fulltext/ED524753.pdf.

40. "About Learning Evaluations," American Council on Education (ACE), 2022, https://www.acenet.edu/Programs-Services/Pages/Credit-Transcripts/About-Learning-Evaluation.aspx.

41. Natalie Schwartz, "Workforce Development, K–12 Teacher Shortages Top List of State Higher Ed Leaders' Concerns," Higher Ed Dive, January 20, 2023. https://www.highereddive.com/news/workforce-development-k-12-teacher-shortages-top-concerns-state-higher-ed-leaders/640805/.

42. Javeria Salman, "Can Apprenticeships Help Alleviate Teacher Shortages?" The Hechinger Report, September 2, 2022, https://hechingerreport.org/can-apprenticeships-help-alleviate-teacher-shortages.

43. Salman, "Can Apprenticeships Help Alleviate Teacher Shortages?"
44. "Fact Sheet: The U.S. Department of Education Announces Partnerships across States, School Districts, and Colleges of Education to Meet Secretary Cardona's Cal to Action to Address the Teacher Shortage," U.S. Department of Education, January 21, 2023, https://www.ed.gov/coronavirus/factsheets/teacher-shortage.
45. "FY 2021 Data and Statistics. Apprenticeship. Employment and Training Administration," U.S. Department of Labor, 2021, https://www.dol.gov/agencies/eta/apprenticeship/about/statistics/2021.
46. NewU, "College That Won't Break the Bank," January 21, 2003, https://newu.university/cost/.
47. Jon Marcus, "Momentum Builds behind a Three-Year Degree to Lower College Costs," *Washington Post*, April 15, 2022. https://www.washingtonpost.com/education/2022/04/15/college-three-year-degree/.
48. Emma Whitford, "A New Push to Create a 3-Year Degree Option," Inside Higher Ed, November 9, 2021, https://www.insidehighered.com/news/2021/11/09/colleges-explore-new-three-year-bachelor%E2%80%99s-degree-program.
49. Whitford, "A New Push to Create a 3-Year Degree Option."
50. Reyna Gobel, "The Benefits of an Accelerated Bachelor's/Master's Degree," Investopedia, December 10, 2022, https://www.investopedia.com/articles/professionaleducation/11/accelerated-bachelors-masters-degree.asp.
51. "Overview: Spring 2022 Enrollment Estimates," National Student Clearinghouse Research Center, Spring 2022, https://nscresearchcenter.org/wp-content/uploads/CTEE_Report_Spring_2022.pdf.
52. Dan Cullinan and Elizabeth Kopko, "Lessons from Two Experimental Studies of Multiple Measures Assessment," Center for the Analysis of Postsecondary Readiness, January 2022, https://postsecondaryreadiness.org/wp-content/uploads/2022/01/multiple-measures-assessment-reflections.pdf.
53. Di Xu, John Fink, and Sabrina Solanki, "College Acceleration for All? Mapping Racial/Ethnic Gaps in Advanced Placement and Dual Enrollment Participation," *American Educational Research Journal* 58, no. 5 (2021): 954–92.
54. "Research on Dual and Concurrent Enrollment Student Outcomes," National Alliance of Concurrent Enrollment Partnerships (NACEP), https://www.nacep.org/resource-center/research-on-dual-and-concurrent-enrollment-student-outcomes/.
55. "Lighting the Path to Remove Systemic Barriers in Higher Education and Award Earned. Postsecondary Credentials through IHFP's Degrees When Due Initiative," Institute for Higher Education Policy (IHEP), May 2022, https://www.ihep.org/publication/lighting-the-path-degrees-when-due/.
56. Liam L. Knox, "Can High Schoolers Save the Community College?" Inside Higher Ed., November 22, 2022, https://www.insidehighered.com/news/2022/11/22/community-colleges-struggle-dual-enrollment-grows.
57. Sarah Hooker, "Addressing a Major Barrier to Dual Enrollment Strategies to Staff Up and Scale Up," Jobs for the Future, March 2019, https://files.eric.ed.gov/fulltext/ED598308.pdf.
58. Elizabeth Kopko, Jessica Brathwaite, and Julia Raufman, *"*The Next Phase of Placement Reform: Moving Toward Equity-Centered Practice,*"* Center for the

Analysis of Postsecondary Readiness, August 2022, https://postsecondaryreadiness.org/next-phase-placement-reform-equity-centered-practice/.

59. Steven Johnson, "In the Rush to Meet Labor Market Needs, Universities Can't Forget the Human Element," *Times Higher Education*, December 2022, https://www.timeshighereducation.com/campus/rush-meet-labour-market-needs-universities-cant-forget-human-element.

Chapter Five

Understanding Today's Student

If they can get you asking the wrong questions, they don't have to worry about answers.

—Thomas Pynchon, Gravity's Rainbow

The COVID-19 pandemic has been hard on everyone with younger adults and traditional-aged college students especially impacted. Between 2020 and 2022, over 1 million students vanished from U.S. colleges and universities.[1] This was due to a variety of factors.

Here are the top five reasons cited for not attending postsecondary education in fall 2021:

- Educational expenses and changes to income from the pandemic
- Had COVID-19 or concerned about contracting the virus
- Uncertainty about classes and/or program changes due to the pandemic
- Content or format of classes changed from in-person to online
- Financial aid changed[2]

While undergraduate enrollments continue to show a decline, one year later the rate of decline appears to have slowed to pre-pandemic rates with an approximately 1 percent decline in undergraduates for fall 2022. Since 2020, the total two-year decline hovered just under 5 percent.[3]

Graduate education, which had seen distinct increases during the pandemic, also showed a 1 percent decline in fall 2022, which may indicate more graduate-level students left their studies to return to the workplace.[4]

Enrollments fell most dramatically during the pandemic within the nation's community colleges. Given that most community colleges are open-enrollment and serve a wide number of students in terms of interest and program type, as well as offer opportunity to many who are on the lower end of the socioeconomic strata, a decline of nearly 25 percent during the height of the pandemic significantly impacted community colleges who educate approximately 40 percent of total college students.[5]

Fortunately for these institutions and the students they serve, as of fall 2022, even community colleges were experiencing positive gains.[6] Declines slowed due to dual-enrolled high school students; and graduating high school seniors and those aged eighteen to twenty years also brought about the increase.[7]

While colleges and universities are presently attempting a "business as usual approach," enrollments continue to stress even the most tenable college administrator. COVID-19 has not helped, but trouble has been on the educational horizon even before the pandemic hit in spring 2020.

Both undergraduate and graduate education have seen declining enrollments since around 2012, losing about 1 percent of students per year.[8] In addition, there is an "enrollment cliff" set to occur in 2025 when the U.S. college-age population is projected to decline by 15 percent for four years or until 2029 due to a decline in birthrates that occurred between 2008 and 2011 in response to the global financial crisis.[9]

During the COVID-19 pandemic, colleges saw another major decline in births during 2020, which will begin reaching colleges by 2037.[10]

While this may appear a nationwide issue, it does not appear as though all colleges and universities will share equally in seeing less students. Demand for elite colleges and universities is projected to remain high because they serve a very small niche market of students while less selective institutions in the Northeast are projected to be impacted the most with regards to declining enrollments.[11]

There are some bright spots occurring within enrollments in higher education, notably that undergraduate enrollment at historically Black colleges and universities are on the rise as well as in primarily online institutions.[12]

In addition, over 50 percent of students who stopped attending due to the pandemic are considering reenrolling, and 40 percent of adults surveyed who had never attended college indicated an interest in an associate degree or certificate.[13]

Beyond a shrinking high school base, the pandemic, and forthcoming "enrollment cliffs," higher education is presently grappling with some serious student concerns that may bring about a potential shift in institutional practices.

THE VALUE OF A COLLEGE DEGREE

At present, there is a growing skepticism for a four-year college degree coupled with the time and effort required to obtain a degree.[14] Add to that the financial cost of college and student debt along with current low unemployment in the U.S. economy and the result has been many students looking for alternatives beyond the traditional four-year or even two-year degree.

Unfortunately, what most students or potential students of higher education do not see is the long-term view in obtaining a college degree, both in terms of personal as well as societal benefits. If this trend continues, experts say it is likely to lessen individual quality of life and the global economic competitiveness of the United States.[15]

As such, this is not just a micro or individual issue, but also a macro and general economic concern as well. It is projected that over the next decade, the United States could see a skills shortage resulting from lack of higher education of between 6 to 8 million employees or roughly 5 percent of the estimated 2029 labor force, which calculates out to about $1.2 trillion in lost economic output if these shortages materialize.[16]

Advanced education and skill development beyond the high school diploma are necessary to meet labor force needs and minimize loss of innovation and creativity needed to move the nation forward. College-educated workers add value to the economy and postsecondary education helps to upskill workers and increase invention coupled with problem solving across industries.[17]

WHY COLLEGE MATTERS

In the United States, as in other countries, postsecondary institutions have contributed to twenty-first-century advancements in technology, science, medicine, and literature due to the longstanding goal to educate people so that they can contribute positively to society.

This has traditionally been done within a broader liberal arts curriculum that is grounded in humanistic inquiry using critical thinking skills in reading, writing, and discussion. Focused around natural and social sciences, as well as the humanities and the arts, the liberal arts education elevates and strengthens the cultural and social awareness of students to consider the complex world around them in holistic and applied ways.

Ultimately, it teaches students how to think broadly and critically so that they can analyze and navigate through complex issues.

College is more than just job training. In the present day, for example, in the United States there is a need for more K–12 teachers and cybersecurity analysts, as well as nurses and engineers. While this specific manner of advanced and technical training can—and is—provided on the college campus, higher education is much more than simply training for a profession.

Beyond the technical acumen, a college degree provides greater opportunity to succeed in a chosen profession with increased access to job opportunities, thereby helping to lessen the divide between those who "have" and "have not" in terms of economic stature and financial means.[18]

In terms of income, the typical college graduate can expect to earn enough relative to a high school graduate by age thirty-three to compensate for being out of the labor force for four years and with borrowing full tuition and fees, books, and supplies.[19]

Lifetime earnings differ by gender, work patterns, geographic location, as well as race and ethnicity. For example, white, non-Hispanic men with a bachelor's degree and working full-time have estimated median lifetime earnings 68 percent higher than for high school graduates.[20]

Even though the pandemic has removed over 1 million students from higher education since March 2020, the "college wage premium" has only gone up with recent college graduates earning, on average, $52,000 per year and young employees with only a high school diploma earning approximately $30,000 per year.[21]

This higher salary is combined with a lower unemployment rate for college graduates compared to high school graduates by half. Taken together, these are both significant economic indicators for why a college education—whether at a two-year college or four-year university—offers more earnings over time and greater economic security than a high school diploma.

While it is generally true that higher education relates to higher earnings, there are many exceptions where some workers earn less despite having more education and some earn more despite having less education.[22] The biggest variability in earnings based on educational degree attainment comes from differences in the field of study and occupation, and these earning gaps widen with age.[23]

Associate-degree recipients earn the most in health practice occupations, followed by computer and mathematical, and then architecture and engineering, whereas for students earning a bachelor's degree, those undergraduate majors leading to the highest-paying careers are in architecture and engineering, followed by computers, statistics, and mathematics, and thirdly majors in business.[24]

RECRUITMENT AND RETENTION

Educational institutions are strategically involved in increasing the number of educated and skilled workers to help develop our knowledge-based economy so that the United States remains competitive in the global marketplace. To do this, colleges must lessen inequities for the individual student to help promote opportunity, as well as work with students to ensure that they secure viable and well-paying employment commensurate with their educational attainment and skill development.

From a diversity and inclusion perspective, America's higher education students struggled during the pandemic with significant declines among men and male students of color.[25] Colleges and universities are working to recruit students of color, as well as those with disabilities, language barriers, and those from low-income backgrounds who faced hardships during the pandemic and who currently have a lack of access to education.[26]

While the pandemic has had a dramatic effect on students pulling away from courses and attending college, there were many students who remained in higher education even with obstacles such as limited or no access to technology, housing insecurity, or food scarcity.

In light of these many challenges, numerous institutions used the relationships built with students to provide needed support remotely or arranged in-person options for students for things like laptop loans, technology access, and temporary housing.

Many campuses focused on relationship building to help with retention and the persistence of students as they work toward graduation. One new freshman relayed that he felt like the "guinea pig generation" because of the lack of stability and the fact that everyone was trying to figure out how to go remote during the pandemic, yet he still felt like his professors "got it" in terms of helping students learn, make friends, and build community.[27]

Post-pandemic multiple approaches to engage students to remain academically active and to connect in the classroom and across the campus community are being emphasized. Accessibility to resources and supports, as well as creating a sense of connectedness across the campus community remains an ongoing goal.

While the pandemic-era enrollment contraction seems to be lessening, trying to bring students back onto campus has been a struggle as many students either left higher education or did not enter at all. Lower enrollments are still generating concern that students who opted out temporarily during the worst of the pandemic may now have permanently moved away from attending higher education at least for the foreseeable future.

Beyond individual virus concerns, this may have been due to losing an income source, deciding to take fewer classes, increased caregiver responsibilities, and/or concern about financial well-being and the need to work.[28] This is particularly concerning for students from lower socioeconomic households.

To lure students back and increase enrollments as well as shore-up retention, various educational institutions are considering a multitude of different strategies, such as reducing tuition costs and lowering textbook prices, ensuring time-to-degree completion, providing additional support for childcare, or offering scholarship assistance.

Some institutions are even considering allowing some leniency in program requirements, such as permitting students to attend less than full-time or take a leave of absence in programs where this traditionally has not been an option.

While colleges and universities are trying to increase recruitment and retention, there are presently conflicting efforts in the U.S. court system to try and limit access to higher education by reducing funding or removing laws that provide protections in support of inclusion and diversity within schools.[29]

Presently there is a percolating ideological discourse about the open exchange of ideas, research, and critical thinking within America's college campuses. This is believed by some to be offensive to their way of thinking.[30] Even though there is widespread agreement that higher education has a wholly positive influence on society, this sentiment is currently being challenged by select groups.[31] This largely political discourse has surfaced post-pandemic placing higher education in the cross hairs of social and cultural change once again.

SOCIAL AND EMOTIONAL SKILLS

Social and emotional learning (SEL) is a process of developing self-awareness, a sense of self-control, and interpersonal skills that help students cope with challenges academically and personally.[32] These relationship skills reflect social awareness and are vital both in and outside of the classroom.

Presently, there is greater emphasis on social and emotional learning as we strive for more equity in education. SEL is defined as the ability to be socially and self-aware.[33] This awareness requires skills, knowledge, and attitudes that help people develop healthy identities, manage emotions, and appreciate different perspectives. In turn, this connects the student to a self-awareness that is caring, engaged, and responsible, and one which can carry over as a lifelong learner in society.[34]

SEL encourages differentiation with respect to student assets and abilities. It respects culture and authenticity, fosters a sense of personal and collective security, and builds on a student's own SEL skills to promote learning. Educators are aware that differentiation is needed in the classroom because a uniform approach does not apply to every student.

Throughout the pandemic, many faculty witnessed structural inequalities that disproportionately affected students of color. Over 50 percent of Latino students and 42 percent of African American students canceled or altered their plans to attend school due to the pandemic. During this same time, only 26 percent of white students changed their plans.[35] Today, there is discussion to find ways to remove systematic barriers.

To close inequities and ensure equal access, all students must feel safe, respected, and empowered. Educational institutions have a responsibility to address inequality by strengthening and developing SEL skills in students, by interrupting inequitable practices, and by aligning academic goals to students' social and emotional development.[36]

The World Economic Forum uses an index to rank social mobility, which is an individual's ability to move either "upward" or "downward" in comparison to their personal circumstances and those of their parents.[37] In the 2020 ranking, Denmark was ranked at number 1 with the United States at 27 out of 82 countries listed in the Global Social Mobility Index.[38]

For higher education in the United States, this data illustrates that, like Demark, we need to create more equitable situations and opportunities for our students. Listening to students' authentic cultural voices and ensuring that the voices of the entire community are present and represented in the classroom is a good start.

McKinsey Global Institute surveyed people in fifteen countries asking what each government should prioritize. The results showed that there were fifty-six foundational skills that benefit citizens with the top seven as follows:

- logical reasoning,
- skills to operate in a digital environment,
- time management with an ability to prioritize,
- understanding biases,
- asking good questions,
- ability to listening actively, and
- to continually learn.[39]

SEL skills and attitudes are needed in the classroom, within institutional leadership, and throughout the campus community, as well as in local communities and in the world of work.

Education is considered by many a basic human right that aids in developing an educated populace that in turn has a positive effect on social capital, responsible citizenship, general emotional and personal well-being, and overall economic productivity.[40]

When more students become formally educated, the pillars of an educated society are continually strengthened. This in turn promotes lifelong learning and continued advancement.

Today more than ever, employers seek employees that have an interpersonal disposition to self-manage and self-regulate. With these aptitudes, employees must be self-aware so that they can work on complex problems with diverse viewpoints and navigate new ideas to continually support and affirm the assets of all members of a team to validate lived experiences, no matter—and in celebration of—their diversity and cultural ways of knowing.

These social and emotional skills transfer to a vocation by providing students with opportunities to navigate through new situations, improve their communication skills with classmates, work in teams, and develop a sense of academic empowerment and personal self-confidence. They develop skills and knowledge to help make complex decisions as well as align to ethical practice that promotes integrity and honesty in their professional activities.

Employers identify the need for social and emotional competence as a necessary requirement in today's marketplace believing that SEL skills and knowledge are just as important as critical thinking, creative thinking, and complex problem-solving skills.[41]

In the classroom, this is conveyed by encouraging teamwork, providing opportunities to practice positive communication skills such as listening, conflict resolution, cooperation, being aware of and resisting stereotypes, considering diverse ideas and viewpoints, communicating effectively, and through sharing one's own thoughts and feelings appropriately.[42]

As students work on problems individually and in diverse groups with guidance from the instructor, they can develop greater social awareness and global competence to work with students from cultures and ethnic backgrounds that might differ from their own, thereby developing a more sophisticated collective understanding as well as fuller academic and professional potential.[43]

STUDENT RESILIENCE

For students who have returned to campus and for those who persisted, educators remain focused on student mental health. Post-pandemic, many colleges and universities have been more intentional about providing students with services such as support groups, therapy and counseling, and disability advocacy. Institutions are normalizing the conversation around mental health across the campus to promote student well-being, mitigate stress, and provide needed social and emotional supports.[44]

Faculty also express this renewed focus on social and emotional learning as they grapple with student learning loss. We have seen a shift by caring faculty toward learning approaches that focus on building strong relationships and collaboration to help students thrive.[45]

To teach today's student using pedagogical best practices and manage learning loss in the classroom, more faculty are providing increased opportunities for students to develop and refine higher-level thinking skills by taking more control over their own learning using inquiry as a learning strategy, explicit instruction that includes interactive lectures, and having students directly apply what is being learned through application and practice around realistic problems.[46]

Within the classroom, many faculty are using models that help build relationships such as restorative circles to create safe spaces to support students when learning difficult material and to consider ways to master material by thinking critically and problem solving.

In this circle, everyone's perspective is heard and by working collaboratively, students build skills that will help them work through conflict and listen to other viewpoints and ideas, while also helping to build a sense of community within the classroom environment.[47]

To support students' well-being and promote resilience, faculty are ensuring that learning gaps are overcome while at the same time providing opportunity, ensuring equity, and celebrating diversity, all while being inclusive in the classroom and teaching content knowledge.

A major goal of formal education has been to impart knowledge and understanding. This is supported using curricular goals. Students continually upgrade their skills and knowledge throughout a lifelong learning process and grow individually as societal needs evolve.

Additionally, educators are constantly considering ways to be approachable to their students. How to support them as they learn and grow from their experiences and recognizing the most critical issues facing students in the present.

While some would argue that it is the student who is changing in the face of higher education rather than the educational institution itself, others would assert that the changing role of education has forced the students to evolve.

Still others find that the changing dynamics of the bond between students and their educational endeavors appear to be evolving in light of technology, current events, and globalization. Even though things appear complicated, for some educators and students alike, the process of teaching and learning is quite straightforward.

Professors teach because they enjoy their discipline and the opportunities that education provides to share their expertise with a broader audience, whether that is by working with students or in research with colleagues. Students learn because they are interested in the subject matter, and they come into a course prepared to be engaged and involved in their own learning.

This simple willingness to learn and openness to new knowledge is the conduit that will move students forward with resilience and tenacity in an age of dizzying new technologies and multiple demands on their time and energy.

This aligns with a growth mindset, coined by Carol Dweck, in which students acknowledge the challenge to change and grow through application and experience.[48] Abilities and intellect are not fixed but can improve through teaching and learning when the student comes into a class or starts a program with a willingness to embrace new experiences and the understanding that there is worthwhile knowledge to be consumed.[49] This is especially true as faculty continue to incorporate practices that are student-centered and help build learner success.

Within higher education, there is a push toward resiliency. To learn from past experiences and move toward sustainable growth and change. Growth that advances higher education to not only meet today's challenges but also adapt to the future challenges of tomorrow.

Resilience through Presence

Presence is important both in a face-to-face classroom and in an online course taught at a distance. A sense of presence, whether it is perceived or tangible, connects the learning community together.[50]

More and more, faculty are moving away from the teacher "sage on the stage" lecturer role toward a more participatory teaching style. This guiding and mentorship approach helps students become more independent thinkers to meet the challenges of today and into the future.[51]

At the center of this type of facilitative learning experience is the intentional creation and support of relationships, which has been a core instructional design component.[52] Diversity of experiences, thought, and ideas continue to be emphasized as educators work with students both cooperatively and collaboratively in the classroom.

Beyond subject-level knowledge, the goal is to help students foster resilience and self-efficacy that they can then take with them beyond the classroom or degree. Building resilience is difficult in the best of times, but in challenging times like a global pandemic, a concerted effort needs to be made by the faculty member and the institution and then continually improved upon.

Throughout the pandemic, emphasis was placed on providing students with flexibility, encouraging well-being, helping to define goals, and developing skills to solve problems. Using this goal-setting approach, students felt that they had more control over their own learning.[53]

When challenges occurred, students were encouraged to see possibilities of failure as learning opportunities and were given opportunities to self-correct and reengage.[54]

While teaching remotely and online throughout the pandemic, many educators found ways to strengthen student relationships by increasing collaboration and community within the online classroom. This allowed for interpersonal connections to be built between students and the instructor, along with improving important concepts and skills needed for students to learn and achieve course learning goals.

MOVING FORWARD

The focus of this chapter was on understanding the current student post-pandemic. A lot has changed over the past couple of years and students are different today than they were pre-pandemic. There are shifting student expectations in higher education in terms of the value of education and why students show up to college in the first place.

Students want to feel supported and be engaged in their quest for knowledge in the classroom and throughout the college campus as well as after graduation. Social and emotional learning offers valuable insights into improving student self-confidence and social skills to develop constructive relationships with others.

Students are resilient and while mental health will remain an issue, the students *want to be all right*. They are attending college to prepare or advance in careers, work toward life goals, and take a more active role toward change efforts. Reimaging education post-pandemic can help students meet their goals and make-up for pandemic related losses.

NOTES

1. Elissa Nadworny, "The College Enrollment Drop Is Finally Letting Up: That's the Good News," National Public Radio, October 20, 2022, https://www.npr.org/2022/10/20/1129980557/the-college-enrollment-drop-is-finally-letting-up-thats-the-good-news.

2. "Impact of the Coronavirus Pandemic on Fall Plans for Postsecondary Education," National Center for Education Statistics, 2022, https://nces.ed.gov/programs/coe/indicator/tpb.

3. "Overview: Spring 2022 Enrollment Estimates," National Student Clearinghouse Research Center, Spring 2022, https://nscresearchcenter.org/wp-content/uploads/CTEE_Report_Spring_2022.pdf.

4. "Overview: Spring 2022 Enrollment Estimates."

5. Jill Barshay, "COVID-19 Has Been Bad for College Enrollment—But Awful for Community College Students," The Hechinger Report, October 2020, https://hechingerreport.org/high-school-graduates-shun-college-in-the-covid-fall-of-2020/.

6. Audrey Williams June, "Higher Ed's Enrollment Fell Again This Fall, If a Bit More Slowly," *The Chronicle of Higher Education*, October 2022, https://www.chronicle.com/article/higher-eds-enrollment-fell-again-this-fall-if-a-bit-more-slowly.

7. "Overview: Spring 2022 Enrollment Estimates."

8. Nadworny, "The College Enrollment Drop Is Finally Letting Up."

9. Paul Copley and Edward Douthett, "Mega-Universities, COVID-19, and the Changing Landscapes of U.S. Colleges," *The CPA Journal*, October 2020.

10. Ray Schroeder, "A Second Demographic Cliff Adds to Urgency for Change," Inside HigherEd, May 2021, https://www.insidehighered.com/digital-learning/blogs/online-trending-now/second-demographic-cliff-adds-urgency-change.

11. Jill Barshay, "College Students Predicted to Fall by More than 15% after the Year 2025," The Hechinger Report, September 10, 2018, https://hechingerreport.org/college-students-predicted-to-fall-by-more-than-15-after-the-year-2025/.

12. Nadworny, "The College Enrollment Drop Is Finally Letting Up."

13. Karin Fischer, "The Shrinking of Higher Ed," *The Chronicle of Higher Education*, August 12, 2022, https://www-chronicle-com.umw.idm.oclc.org/article/the-shrinking-of-higher-ed.

14. Stephanie Saul, "College Enrollment Drops, Even as the Pandemic's Effects Ebb," *The New York Times,* May 26, 2022, https://www.nytimes.com/2022/05/26/us/college-enrollment.html.

15. Jon Marcus, "How Higher Education Lost Its Shine," The Hechinger Report, August 2022, https://hechingerreport.org/how-higher-education-lost-its-shine/.

16. Douglas Holtz-Eakin and Tom Lee, "Projecting Future Skill Shortages through 2029," American Action Forum, July 18, 2019, https://www.americanactionforum.org/research/projecting-future-skill.

17. Anthony P. Carnevale and Stephen J. Rose, "The Economy Goes to College: The Hidden Promise of Higher Education in the Post-Industrial Service Economy," Georgetown University Center on Education and The Workforce, 2015, https://cew-georgetown.wpenginepowered.com/wp-content/uploads/EconomyGoesToCollege.pdf.

18. Anthony P. Carnevale, Tamara Jayasundera, and Artem Gulish, "America's Divided Recovery: College Haves and Have-Nots," Georgetown University Center on Education and the Workforce, 2016, https://cewgeorgetown.wpenginepowered.com/wp-content/uploads/Americas-Divided-Recovery-web.pdf.

19. Jennnifer Ma, Matea Pender, and Meredith Welch, "Education Pays 2019," College Board, 2019, https://research.collegeboard.org/trends/education-pays/report-archive.

20. Sandy Baum, Charles Kurose, and Jennifer Ma, "How College Shapes Lives: Understanding the Issues," College Board, October 2013, https://research.collegeboard.org/media/pdf/education-pays-how-college-shapes-lives-report.pdf.

21. Chris Geary, "College Pays Off. But By How Much Depends on Race, Gender, and Type of Degree," New America, March 1, 2022, https://www.newamerica.org/education-policy/edcentral/college-pays-off/.

22. Anthony P. Carnevale, Ban Cheah, and Emma Wenzinger, "The College Payoff: More Education Doesn't Always Mean More Earnings," Georgetown University Center on Education and the Workforce, 2021, https://cewgeorgetown.wpengine-powered.com/wp-content/uploads/cew-college_payoff_2021-fr.pdf.

23. Carnevale et al., "The College Payoff."

24. Carnevale, et al., "The College Payoff."

25. Rachel Kidman, Rachel Margolis, Emily Smith-Greenaway, and Ashton M. Verdery, "Estimates and Projections of COVID-19 and Parental Death in the US," *JAMA Pediatrics* 175, no. 7 (2021): 745–46.

26. "The 2020 Annual Homeless Assessment Report (AHAR) to Congress," U.S. Department of Housing and Urban Development Office of Community Planning and Development, January 2021, https://www.huduser.gov/portal/sites/default/files/pdf/2020-AHAR-Part-1.pdf.

27. Amy Morona, Daniel Perez, Emma Folts, and Ian Hodgson, "'We Were the Guinea Pig Generation': How the Pandemic Shaped Current College Freshmen," February 1, 2023, *Open Campus*, https://www.opencampusmedia.org/2023/02/01/we-were-the-guinea-pig-generation-how-the-pandemic-shaped-current-college-freshmen/.

28. "Education in a Pandemic: The Disparate Impacts of COVID-19 on America's Students," Department of Education Office for Civil Rights, June 9, 2021, https://www2.ed.gov/about/offices/list/ocr/docs/20210608-impacts-of-covid19.pdf.

29. Sébastien Goudeau, Camille Sanrey, Arnaud Stanczak, Antony Manstead, and Céline Darnon, "Why Lockdown and Distance Learning during the COVID-19 Pandemic Are Likely to Increase the Social Class Achievement Gap," *Nature Human Behaviour* 5 (2021): 1273–81.

30. Joe Pinsker, "Republicans Changed Their Mind about Higher Education Really Quickly," *The Atlantic*, August 21, 2019, https://www.theatlantic.com/education/archive/2019/08/republicans-conservatives-college/596497/.

31. Kim Parker, "The Growing Partisan Divide in Views of Higher Education," Pew Research Center, August 19, 2019, https://www.pewresearch.org/social-trends/2019/08/19/the-growing-partisan-divide-in-views-of-higher-education-2/.

32. "Fundamentals of SEL," CASEL: Collaborative for Academic, Social, and Emotional Learning, January 22, 2023, https://casel.org/fundamentals-of-sel/.

33. "Fundamentals of SEL."

34. "Fundamentals of SEL."

35. "Public Viewpoint: COVID-19 Work and Education Survey," Strada Center for Consumer Insights, June 10, 2020, https://www.stradaeducation.org/wp-content/uploads/2020/06/Public-Viewpoint-Report-Week-9.pdf.

36. Rebecca Bailey, Emily A. Meland, Gretchen Brion-Meisels, and Stephanie M. Jones, "Getting Developmental Science Back into Schools: Can What We Know about Self-Regulation Help Change How We Think about 'No Excuses'?" *Frontiers Psychology* 10 (2019), https://www.frontiersin.org/articles/10.3389/fpsyg.2019.01885/full.

37. "Global Social Mobility Index 2020: Why Economies Benefit from Fixing Inequality," World Economic Forum, January 19, 2020, https://www.weforum.org/reports/global-social-mobility-index-2020-why-economies-benefit-from-fixing-inequality/.

38. "The Global Social Mobility Report 2020," World Economic Forum, January 2020, https://www3.weforum.org/docs/Global_Social_Mobility_Report.pdf.

39. Macro Dondi, Julia Klier, Frédéric Panier, and Jörg Schubert, "Defining the Skills Citizens Will Need in the Future World of Work," McKinsey & Company, June 21, 2021, https://www.mckinsey.com/industries/public-and-social-sector/our-insights/defining-the-skills-citizens-will-need-in-the-future-world-of-work?

40. Sylvia Schmelke, "Recognizing and Overcoming Inequity in Education," *United Nations Chronicle*, January 22, 2020, https://www.un.org/en/un-chronicle/recognizing-and-overcoming-inequity-education.

41. "Annual Report 2021–2022," World Economic Forum, September 7, 2022, https://www.weforum.org/reports/annual-report-2021-2022.

42. Joseph A. Durlak, Roger P. Weissberg, Allison B. Dymnicki, and Rebecca D. Taylor, "The Impact of Enhancing Students' Social and Emotional Learning: A

Meta-Analysis of School-Based Universal Interventions," *Child Development* 82, no. 1 (2011): 405–32.

43. "To Achieve Equity in Education," The National Equity Project, 2022, https://www.nationalequityproject.org/.

44. Naz Beheshti, "We Can No Longer Ignore Burnout Syndrome Related to Chronic Stress, Says World Health Organization," *Forbes*, June 10, 2019, https://www.forbes.com/sites/nazbeheshti/2019/06/10/we-can-no-longer-ignore-burnout-syndrome-related-to-chronic-stress-says-world-health-organization/?sh=76599cd56a37.

45. Carla Evans, "Instructing and Assessing 21st Century Skills: A Focus on Collaboration," Center for Assessment, November 13, 2021, https://www.nciea.org/blog/instructing-assessing-21st-century-skills-a-focus-on-collaboration/.

46. Johanna Alonso, "How Higher Ed Can Help Remedy K–12 Learning Loss," Inside Higher Ed, October 26, 2022, https://www.insidehighered.com/news/2022/10/26/colleges-can-help-k-12-schools-combat-pandemic-learning-loss.

47. Larry Ferlazzo, "Ways to Implement Restorative Practices in the Classroom," *Education Week*, January 9, 2020, https://www.edweek.org/teaching-learning/opinion-ways-to-implement-restorative-practices-in-the-classroom/2020/01.

48. Carol S. Dweck, *Mindset: The New Psychology of Success* (New York: Ballantine Books, 2016).

49. Jonathan Malesic, "The Key to Success in College Is So Simple, It's Almost Never Mentioned," *The New York Times*, January 2023, https://www.nytimes.com/2023/01/03/opinion/college-learning-students-success.html.

50. Liam Rourke and Heather Kanuka, "Learning in Communities of Inquiry: A Review of the Literature," *Journal of Distance Education* 23, no. 1 (2009): 19–48.

51. Alyson Klien, "Tech Struggles during COVID-19 Hurting Students' Ability to Learn, Educators Say," *Education Week*, September 24, 2020, https://www.edweek.org/education/tech-struggles-during-covid-19-hurting-students-ability-to-learn-educators-say/2020/09.

52. Atsusi Hirumi, *Grounded Designs for Online and Hybrid Learning: Design Fundamentals*, International Society for Technology Education (Eugene Oregon, 2014).

53. Robert J. Marzano, *Designing and Teaching Learning Goals and Objectives: Classroom Strategies That Work* (Denver, CO: Marzano Research Laboratory, 2009).

54. Amy C. Edmondson, "Strategies for Learning from Failure," *Harvard Business Review*, April 2011, https://hbr.org/2011/04/strategies-for-learning-from-failure.

Chapter Six

Collaboration and Community

If you want to go fast, go alone. If you want to go far, go together.

—African Proverb

This chapter explores collaboration and how it can be used in a classroom and with a community of learners. The goal is to build a thinking classroom and celebrate the diversity of the class through engagement and continued collaboration while strengthening complex thinking skills around course topics to extend and grow student knowledge and understanding.

Moving forward post-pandemic, students are being exposed to new and different experiences and diverse people. They are problem solving in more applied ways and with greater real-world application than was possible during the throes of the COVID-19 pandemic when learning was more isolated and virtual.[1]

THE TRADITIONAL CLASSROOM

Traditional education follows the early seventeenth-century teachings of philosopher John Locke who believed that we are born with a mind that is a *tabula rasa*. Loosely translated this means we are a "blank" or "clean slate" with no rules given to help us process or think more deeply about information. As a result, we use emotions to help us sift through new information, and we react to this information using our emotions.[2]

If we carry this premise into the classroom, it follows that students need to be told about how to interpret concepts, processes, and ideas. To construct more complex knowledge in the traditional classroom, students must listen, take notes, and then memorize. Thus, the practice of traditional teaching is one in which instructors directly transfer their expert knowledge to students.

This type of learning assumes that the instructor controls the selection of material, organizes the learning, and transmits to students what they should know, do, and understand. The student is not expected to come into the classroom with prior knowledge or experience.

Paulo Freire referred to this as the "banking method" of education and criticized what he viewed as its oppressive nature, for example, a vertical relationship where the teacher is the depositor of knowledge, and the student is the willing and passive receiver.[3] There is no outlet for collaboration in the traditional classroom model.

Early instruction created a system of school where the instructor knows everything, and the role of the student is to listen and remember. It is an isolative process with little social interactions and substantial emphasis on independent work.

This type of instruction was illustrated as far back as the fourteenth century by Laurentius de Voltolina.[4] In it, you see an attentive class sitting in rows all facing the front of the classroom to listen to the instructor lecturing. The role of the student was to pay attention and absorb information.

This image depicts what higher education has often looked like. Traditionally, students funnel into lecture-based classrooms to listen to an instructor deliver a lecture sometimes with a visual presentation. Generally, material is summarized and focused on key vocabulary, concepts, and principles important for students to remember.[5] Students are expected to take notes on the information and extract or reproduce the information during planned written assessments.

Within this traditional model, learning is centered within the classroom and is independent and singular. There is minimal student agency and little opportunity for students to make their own learning choices or develop lifelong skills and habits of mind beyond what is being taught.

THE COLLABORATIVE CLASSROOM

Beyond the traditional classroom, Freire promoted a more equitable model where neither the instructor nor the student is above the other and there is mutual respect.[6] This can be seen in the collaborative classroom where the focus is on dialog, action, and reflection.

By utilizing collaborative rather than traditional learning strategies, students become responsible for their learning and authors of their own education.[7] A common theme of collaborative learning is having students work together on a shared learning task.

Activities in a collaborative classroom can vary widely and include:

- group discussions,
- peer editing,
- case studies,
- simulations,
- games, and
- role play.[8]

The one common thread of learning collaboratively is that students perform the exploration and application of the course material and are not led or directed by the instructor in the presentation or exploration.[9]

The instructor functions more as a facilitator and students must be active participants in their own learning. This experience connects students to the understandings of others, develops higher order thinking skills, and increases retention.

When using cooperative groups, students similarly work together in the pursuit of a joint educational effort. What they are working toward may also vary, but cooperative learning is more structured than collaborative learning and involves small group learning around precisely defined tasks or problems.[10] It can be geared toward problem solving, or it can focus on "making" and creating.[11] Both cooperative and collaborative learning combine academic knowledge with social learning experiences.

COLLABORATIVE LEARNING IN PRACTICE

To make collaborative learning most effective, several assumptions about students and the process of learning are necessary:

- Learning is active and constructive. Students create something new.
- Learning is dependent on rich contexts. Students solve problems.
- Learning is social and centered around mutual engagement, exploration, meaning making, and feedback.
- There is not a one-size-fits-all approach. Students are diverse in background, learning styles, and experiences.[12]

Working collaboratively, students learn how to be knowledge creators. They own the information or content developed through their involvement with classmates. In coordination with others, the skills learned are applied to the larger society whether in the workplace or community.

Collaborative Teams

In collaborative teams, students work together in meaningful ways in a small group setting to achieve course learning goals. Students are accountable to one another and to the team as a whole to be successful. Students organize their own efforts and group performance resulting in group synergy based on the interdependence among the various team members.[13]

Building and strengthening teamwork skills enables students to learn soft skills. They practice and develop decision making, adaptability, flexibility, and problem solving as they engage with others different than themselves. Utilizing collaborative teams allows students to work together in an immersive experience where deep learning is possible to achieve the following three components:

- *Mastery* or the development of knowledge and skill
- *Identity* and seeing the core self as connected to learning and doing
- *Creativity* or the act of producing something[14]

FROM COLLABORATION TO COMMUNITY

Community is at the heart of higher education. Colleges and universities serve as one of the best examples of a learning community. Colleges continually seek opportunities for relationship and community building whether it is online or face-to-face, or some combination. Whole community collaboration connects students to the campus and builds relationships.

According to Lev Vygotsky, an early twentieth-century developmental psychologist, these social interactions build students' cognitive development. As a result, they are able to work at higher intellectual levels in a collaborative community than when working independently.[15]

During the pandemic, faculty attempted to incorporate social approaches by making small adaptations to their pedagogy to try and connect learning activities as they went from the in-person classroom to the computer screen and online teaching.[16]

These socially oriented activities helped to foster skills of self-resilience and connected students through a mutual motivation to learn and share. In addition, understanding that everything took more time when performed online versus being in-class was an important adjustment as was lessening expectations for how much content could be covered and how quickly.

Also, students in general just really needed to talk.[17] Students *wanted* to collaborate and connect with faculty and their classmates. This was especially true at the beginning of the pandemic when everything was so uncertain.

Students wanted to be asked how they were doing and what was going on in their world. This type of connection was essential to confirming the community that had already been created in the former in-person class as well as helped students retain a sense of normalcy that the instructor and the students still cared about each other.

Creating routines and connecting the varied cultures of students within assignments and class activities helped students feel emotionally safe and part of a community of learners.[18]

As challenges come up outside the context of the classroom, the classroom community can be a place to come together for unity and sharing. Through this community-building, students are able to establish networks and relationships with their fellow students and the instructor.

Post-pandemic, faculty recognize the need to rebuild a sense of collaboration as well as advance skills needed by students to work through complex problems. Deprived of normal day-to-day social interactions during the pandemic, strategies that develop and strengthen students' social and emotional learning are needed to help students reconnect.[19]

While social and team collaboration skills may be out of practice, these skills come back relatively easily when put into use as students reemerge back into classrooms, residence halls, and campus meeting spaces. At present, many students are making friends, talking to people, and spending time socializing, thereby quickly improving their communication, collaboration, and social skills.

Restorative Circles

Restorative circles introduced at the beginning of class can help provide students with needed social and emotional support as well as build capacity for forming deeper and more complex relationships.

Students can discuss personal and/or professional challenges they are facing in an open and safe space while also engaging in important listening and problem-resolution strategies with peers to develop communication, build relationship skills, and form personal bonds.[20]

During the pandemic, utilizing virtual restorative circles provided opportunities for students to visualize new perspectives, challenge their own thinking, and provide—as well as receive—needed support.[21] This sense of collegiality and team support connected students to the community of the classroom and built stronger networks for students both inside and outside of the classroom during a very challenging time.

Reintroducing this best practice into the current classroom can provide an important "check-in" for the instructor to determine how students are doing in terms of their social and emotional health at any given point during the course. It also allows students time to reflect on their day or week and share experiences with others in similar ways.

In today's classroom, restorative circles can help build a sense of shared connectedness and provide the motivation and support to more fully participate in the class resulting in improved social skills and overall personal well-being.

Whole Community Engagement

Collaborations can extend outside the campus as well. This is especially relevant post-pandemic as more than half of nonprofit organizations experienced issues in 2020 that threatened their long-term financial stability.[22]

Colleges and universities are excellent conduits for students to interact with the local community through project-based learning and other service-learning opportunities. This field-based experiential learning provides students with direct experience about issues and problems they are currently studying that exist in the real world.[23]

In a problem-focused approach, students in a social entrepreneurship class may partner with a local nonprofit organization to solve a communications problem. The solution may be to develop a more robust social media platform to improve community engagement. With project-based learning and working in small groups, a business class may help local businesses complete a business plan or refine a marketing plan.

Service learning combines the educational benefits of project-based and problem-focused learning with the added benefit of community service to tackle real-life problems in the community.

Service learning is a credit-based educational experience undertaken as part of a class in which students participate in a service activity to further understand and apply the course content.[24] Examples include working with Habitat for Humanity on a building site, packing food supplies for the homeless, cleaning up a local highway, tutoring at-risk youth, or launching a water awareness campaign.[25]

In addition to being out and in the community, students complete research on the issues at hand and the project to be undertaken. They may do culminating presentations or weekly discussions of progress with the rest of the class.

Reflection is an important component of community-based engagement projects where students actively and critically reflect about themselves, the project, and how they will think differently going forward about the issue(s) at hand.

On the campus itself, there may be networking opportunities, guest speakers, career fairs, or performances. Colleges are looking for ways to be sustainable and stay relevant in this current post-pandemic world. Creating more opportunities to collaborate with the real world disrupts the traditional learning environment of the solitary classroom and allows for greater connections and networking opportunities to be built between departments, classrooms, and the broader campus community.

COMMUNITY AND CONNECTEDNESS

As institutions reestablish a sense of community on their campuses and in the higher education classroom, it is important to consider student connectedness. This relates to student participation in a class or project and gives voice to how students define their sense of belonging and overall support.

Belonging is a subjective perception of inclusion, connectedness, and integration in three primary dimensions—social, academic, and institutional.[26] Students feel they belong when they are comfortable in class and have supportive peers and faculty mentors. This connectedness is weakened when there is little class engagement, the student has modest to no peer comradery, and interacting with faculty is minimal to nonexistent.

Connectedness occurs through building community and fostering dialog. This can be experienced in a singular class or through an overall college experience. Students feel more connected to their learning, which in turn allows for greater satisfaction with the course, program, and/or institution.

The overall result is improved retention as students experience a sense of alignment and general fulfillment with the college, program, course, instructor, and other students.

Going forward, colleges should work to ensure that students feel included, accepted, respected, and supported in the learning environment. There are four distinct influences that are necessary to develop a *feeling* of membership within a community:

- one must "feel" that they belong and have an essential role;
- participation within the group makes a significant difference and has some influence;
- through participation, personal needs and wants are achieved; and
- one obtains an emotional connection due to their contribution, which in turn impacts the learning experiences of the group.[27]

The Importance of Relationships

Relationships are central to learning. This formation of a bond between faculty and student, among students themselves, and with others in the community is critical in today's complex and uncertain world.

Today, we are seeing relationship building emphasized within the classroom and through the connection of learning itself. Collaborative learning helps to develop higher-level thinking skills in students and the act of working together boosts self-confidence and self-esteem.[28] This promotes team-building skills, as well as enhances self-resilience. Team projects develop leadership skills and help to improve students social and interpersonal skills by working with people who are different from them.

Teaching students to navigate through the problems of today and helping to prepare students for tomorrow's challenges helps students individually and communities collectively. Student connections are supported, and diverse interactions encouraged for the heterogeneity they bring to the course content and the learning experience.

MOVING FORWARD

Within the collaborative learning environment, emphasis is placed on community building to encourage learning and sharing. Creating an optimal learning environment to bring students together so that they can brainstorm, exchange information, and focus on discovery, understanding, knowledge creation, transmission, transformation, and assimilation of course content adds to and creates value from the educative process.

Through collaboration, teams can work together on challenging problems centered around course learning goals. Within a group learning process, students' complete tasks, create products, and share thinking all while experiencing different ideas and ways of knowing and thinking. Through this process, students are engaged in didactic communication to actively participate in creating new understandings that extend and compliment members of the team and can be transferred to situations outside of the group.[29]

Collaboration, community, and connectedness are good for relationship building. The main purpose for collaborative learning is to provide rich interactive experiences for students to challenge one another's thinking.

Once this is accomplished, students are able to think more critically about the content, exchange information, apply this newly constructed knowledge directly to their own experiences, and then share with the world.

NOTES

1. Leah Campbell, "Impact of COVID-19 on Children's Social Skills," *Forbes*, October 31, 2021, https://www.forbes.com/sites/leahcampbell/2021/10/31/impact-of-covid-19-on-childrens-social-skills.

2. William Uzgalis, "John Locke," The Stanford Encyclopedia of Philosophy, Stanford University, 2022, https://plato.stanford.edu/entries/locke/.

3. Kim Diaz, "Paulo Freire (1921–1997)," Internet Encyclopedia of Philosophy, https://iep.utm.edu/freire/.

4. Laurentius de Voltolina, *Henricus de Alemannia con i suoi student*, Second half of fourteenth-century, painting, height: 7 X 8.6 (inches), https://commons.wikimedia.org/wiki/File:Laurentius_de_Voltolina_001.jpg?_ga=2.57876778.18698870.1671388990-1862814611.1671388990.

5. Wilbert McKeachie and Marilla Svinicki, *Teaching Tips: Strategies, Research, and Theory for College and University Teachers* (Boston: Houghton Mifflin, 2014).

6. Paulo Freire, *Pedagogy of the Oppressed* (New York: Continuum, 1970).

7. Michael Wehmeyer and Yong Zhao, *Teaching Students to Become Self-Determined Learners* (Alexandria, VA: Association for Curriculum and Development, 2020).

8. K. Patricia Cross, Elizabeth F. Barkley, and Claire H. Major, *Collaborative Learning Techniques: A Handbook for College Faculty* (San Francisco, CA: Jossey-Bass, 2014).

9. Barbara Leigh Smith and Jean T. MacGregor, "What Is Collaborative Learning?," in *Collaborative Learning: A Sourcebook for Higher Education* (National Center on Postsecondary Teaching, Learning, and Assessment at Pennsylvania State University, 1982).

10. Anne S. Goodsell, Michelle R. Maher, and Vincent Tinto, *Collaborative Learning: A Sourcebook for Higher Education* (University Park, PA: National Center on Postsecondary Teaching, Learning, and Assessment, 1992).

11. Neil Davidson and Toni Worsham, *Enhancing Thinking through Cooperative Learning* (New York: Teachers College Press, 1992).

12. Goodsell et al., *Collaborative Learning*.

13. Ruth Federman Stein and Sandra Hurd, *Using Student Teams in the Classroom: A Faculty Guide* (Bolton, MA: Anker Publishing, 2000).

14. Jal Mehta and Sarah Fine, *In Search of Deeper Learning: The Quest to Remake the American High School* (Cambridge, MA: Harvard University Press, 2019).

15. Lev S. Vygotsky, *Mind and Society* (Cambridge, MA: Harvard University Press, 1978).

16. Paula MacDowell, "Teachers Designing Immersive Learning Experiences for Environmental and Sustainability Education," in *Immersive Education* (Springer, Cham., 2022), 171–86.

17. Sarah Schwartz, "How to Make Teaching Better: 8 Lessons Learned from Remote and Hybrid Learning," *Education Week*, April 20, 2021, https://www.edweek.org/teaching-learning/how-to-make-teaching-better-8-lessons-learned-from-remote-and-hybrid-learning/2021/04.

18. "Culturally Responsive Teaching: A Guide to Evidence-Based Practices for Teaching All Students Equitably," Education Northwest: Region X Equity Assistance Center, March 2016, https://educationnorthwest.org/sites/default/files/resources/culturally-responsive-teaching.pdf.

19. "2021 Social and Emotional Learning Report," McGraw Hill, 2021, http://mheducation.com/sel-survey.

20. Bob Costello, Joshua Wachetel, and Ted Wachtel, *The Restorative Practices Handbook: For Teachers, Disciplinarians and Administrators* (Bethlehem, PA: International Institute for Restorative Practices, 2009).

21. Gina Baral Abrams and Joshua Wachtel, "During the COVID-19 Crisis, Restorative Practices Can Help," International Institute for Restorative Practices Graduate School, March 24, 2020, https://www.iirp.edu/news/during-the-covid-19-crisis-restorative-practices-can-help.

22. Donella Wilson, "Strategies for Nonprofit Success in a Post-Pandemic Landscape," *Philanthropy News Digest*, June 4, 2021, https://philanthropynewsdigest.org/features/the-sustainable-nonprofit/strategies-for-nonprofit-success-in-a-post-pandemic-landscape.

23. "High-Impact Practices," American Association of Colleges and Universities (AAC&U), January 1, 2023, https://www.aacu.org/trending-topics/high-impact.

24. Robert G. Bringle and Julie A. Hatcher, "Institutionalization of Service Learning in Higher Education," *The Journal of Higher Education* 71, no. 3 (2000), 273–90.

25. Heather Wolpert-Gawron, "What the Heck Is Service Learning?" Edutopia, November 7, 2016, https://www.edutopia.org/blog/what-heck-service-learning-heather-wolpert-gawron.

26. Justin Beauchamp, Emily Schwartz, and Elizabeth Davidson Pisacreta, "Seven Practices for Building Community and Student Belonging Virtually," *The Chronicle of Higher Education*, May 13, 2021, https://www.chronicle.com/professional-development/report/seven-practices-for-building-community-and-student-belonging-virtually.

27. David W. McMillan and David M. Chavis, "Sense of Community: A Definition and Theory," *Journal of Community Psychology* 14, no. 1 (1986), 6–23.

28. Sabrina Gates, "Benefits of Collaboration," National Education Association, October 18, 2018, https://www.nea.org/professional-excellence/student-engagement/tools-tips/benefits-collaboration.

29. Mary Beth Klinger and Teresa Coffman, "Building Knowledge through Dynamic Meta-Communication," in *Meta-Communication for Reflective Conversations: Models for Distance Education* (Hershey, PA: IGI Global, 2012), 135–47.

Chapter Seven

Incorporating Inquiry

I have been impressed with the urgency of doing. Knowing is not enough; we must apply. Being willing is not enough; we must do

—Leonardo da Vinci

John Dewey, an American philosopher and educator, is credited for his work on learning by doing, which laid the initial building blocks for inquiry-based learning used throughout classrooms today.[1] The idea of "productive inquiry" can be used to apply Dewey's beliefs from almost a century ago as we explore a world of constant change and upheaval from the COVID-19 pandemic.

The world is changing so rapidly that traditional education as we now know it will evolve into the next decade and most certainly look much different in the next century. When colleges went virtual at the start of 2020, one of the biggest challenges was finding ways to successfully educate students remotely who normally might not have taken an online course as well as preparing faculty who were ill-prepared to teach in a virtual environment.[2]

There was a need to invest quickly in technologies, such as Web conferencing platforms to provide synchronous opportunities for learning as well as train faculty on how best to facilitate online learning activities and communicate with their classes.

As colleges continued in remote learning throughout 2020 and into 2021, instructors continued to rethink and retool their online teaching methods. Faculty adjusted assignments, became more flexible on due dates, and focused on trying to increase interactions and participation of students in the remote learning environment as the pandemic wore on and classes remained at a distance.

As faculty adapted to using their course management system as a "classroom" and relied on technology as the mechanism for how students would interact with the content and engage with their classmates, they continued to think differently about their teaching. Students were now asked to collaborate using shared documents, assignments were scaffolded to make them more manageable online, and formative feedback loops were created to try and keep students motivated with remote learning.

All of this was done to improve engagement and restore the community of the classroom in the new online environment using technology to guide inquiry.[3] Through an inquiry learning process, educators adjusted their teaching process and evolved how they thought about their teaching practice to improve communication, spur interactions and online engagement, and promote learning in their remote classroom.

CONSTRUCTIVISM

Inquiry is based on empiricism and centers around constructivist learning theory. Constructivism's main premise is that we actively construct knowledge and skills using our own reality through experiences and interactions with the environment.[4]

At its heart, constructivism is a student-centered approach that incorporates both independent work and group work at the same time. It builds upon skills and knowledge and extends student learning through a process of actively planning, organizing, and problem solving to find workable solutions.[5]

Through this approach to knowledge construction, awareness of the world is influenced by our perceptions, interactions, and observations, and we use each to create a sense of experience.[6] John Locke and David Hume, both empiricist philosophers of the seventeenth and eighteenth centuries respectively, believed that our "experiences" are the fundamental source of knowledge and suggested that all our rationally formed beliefs are justifiable because of these experiences with our environment.[7]

Learning requires attention, memorization, and recall as well as understanding.[8] This process takes place over time and is visible through a performance, a change in attitude, behavior, knowledge, or belief.[9] Our previous learning continually informs how we interpret new knowledge and respond to new experiences, either individually or in a social context. Prior experiences can hinder future learning, especially if we do not critically evaluate new knowledge or if we are not willing to change or adjust our own thinking and understandings. As we learn, we organize information in our memory, and later retrieve this information and apply it to new situations.

In the constructivist classroom, the teacher is the facilitator or "guide on the side" rather than the "sage on the stage."[10] Instead of directing or telling students what is to be learned, the instructor guides and facilitates the learning process. Students are challenged to ask difficult questions and to locate quality resources to find solutions around "big idea" questions.[11]

These questions are extremely important because it means that students are cultivating their imagination. In the process, they are active participants in their own learning and are not passive observers of information or content.

There are two main forms of constructivism—cognitive and social. Lev Vygotsky, a social constructivist, suggested that learning evolves through social and cultural interactions, and that students can, with the help of a more experienced peer, master concepts and ideas they could not understand on their own.[12] As learners interact with their environment, they are also interacting with others, which includes other cultures and ways of knowing. These new social experiences help develop deeper thought and an ability to engage in deeper inquiry.[13]

Jean Piaget, a developmental psychologist, proposed the theory of cognitive development believing that individuals construct their own knowledge, which is built through experience and leads to creating individualized mental models that promote learning.[14]

According to the constructivist theory of learning, teaching must offer experiences that:

- provide connections to existing knowledge by adding to students' prior understanding,
- motivate students to be active and self-directed learners,
- offer authentic learning opportunities, and
- comprise collaborative or cooperative learning with students working together in small groups.[15]

KNOWLEDGE CONSTRUCTION

Knowledge construction is a constructivist, inquiry-based, reflective, and collaborative pedagogical process. The premise centers on developing learners that are active constructors of knowledge. When students are active in the learning process, using a knowledge construction approach, they are actively contemplating and transferring new information.

This approach focuses learning on authentic and real-life problems, skill development, and connecting to students' prior knowledge. To help ensure that learning is taking place, continuous assessments are used to both inform students and the instructor about what is being learned and what future learning is needed. Throughout this process, students are encouraged to become more self-regulated and self-aware.

The instructor's role is one of organizing the environment as well as the process of learning. This is done by scaffolding learning activities to help students build needed skills to think more critically to successfully work through the content. By embedding frequent practice, students are guided through the new information and organize it in meaningful ways to connect to previous knowledge. The instructor facilitates this process, helping students develop content knowledge, as well as build on conceptual understanding to promote cooperative learning.[16]

As faculty incorporated various strategies, methods, and technology tools into their newly remote and online classes during the pandemic, they were additionally integrating interactivity, social context, and communication technologies into the course to engage learners in the process of learning.[17] The constructivist model of collaboration, communication, and interactivity came to the forefront of the knowledge construction and course planning process.

As educators incorporate knowledge construction practices into their classrooms post-pandemic, they are using active and social learning, which includes having students interact with classmates, experts in the field, and their own research.

This active learning process, with an emphasis on connecting new knowledge with concepts and information that students have already learned, helps students construct more complex meanings about the new information they are learning about.[18]

CREATIVITY

Creativity is at the heart of inquiry. Creativity is the ability to generate new ideas, alternatives, or possibilities in response to perceived needs and opportunities.[19] Creative traits include originality, open-mindedness, curiosity, persistence, playful attitude, receptiveness to new ideas, and a focused approach to problem solving.[20]

Creative work can benefit individuals, organizations, and societies that invest in it to help solve significant problems faced around the world.[21] Many see creativity as the key to education and the solution for our collective futures.[22] Helping to facilitate an inquisitive mindset and making this a focus in education can help students solve those previously unsolvable "wicked" problems and advance our communities socially and culturally.

While we tend to be prolific with ideas, we often struggle with the development of viable and feasible solutions. Horst Rittel first defined wicked problems and noted that each is unique and interconnected, and there is no one template to follow when solving.[23]

Expertise is the foundation for all creative work and personal motivation and interest are essential to facilitating creative ideas.[24] Along with an individual desire to create is the importance of being in an environment that supports and recognizes creative work. This is where the classroom and organizational culture of the educational institution comes in. There needs to be a fostering of ideas throughout the institution that are free-flowing and support open and constructive creative thought.

IMAGINATION

Play, questioning, and imagination lie at the heart of learning.[25] When the focus is on the whole of educating, it opens the educative process to not just teaching facts but teaching students how to learn and therefore how to create.

Using imagination and play is an effective way for students to learn. Imagination sparks innovation and creativity, necessary components for entrepreneurship and expansion of new ideas in a democratic society. The challenge in education is to find ways to introduce imagination, spur creativity, and foster innovation while delivering on the requirements of course outcomes, curriculum standardization, and content level knowledge.

Much of this text focuses on the need for educational institutions to embrace change and promote innovation moving forward post-pandemic. The same is true for students in terms of seeing the constant evolution of their discipline and the improvements being made in their educative process.

We can ask students to research and report on the known, but additionally we need to challenge them to imagine the impossible and to seek out voices that might not be in the mainstream. Suggesting that students place themselves into novel situations, meet diverse people, and play with ideas or experience thoughts that might be different from their own are important aspects for educational growth. As a college and as a society, we are all better for it.

INQUIRY

Inquiry encourages curiosity. It embodies an eagerness and an interest to speculate, investigate, ask tough questions, and challenge one's—as well as others—thinking and understanding. The goal within inquiry learning is to continually improve ideas and systems through this challenge process.

In the learning practice, inquiry is predicated through questioning. The result is the development of new ideas and the connecting of these ideas with others in new and unique ways. Using inquiry, students pursue new ways of thinking by asking open-ended questions and working through an iterative process.

The art of inquiry is that it is hands-on, practical, flexible, creative, and involves investigation as well as imagination. Meaningful and thoughtful connections are made by asking questions, conducting research, and articulating informed decisions that are authentic to the problems being solved. This type of real-world problem solving is precisely what is needed to help solve the many issues and challenges that exist in the world today.

The inquiry process is a continuous interaction with the environment and an exploration that involves discovering and experiencing to pose original and essential questions. The learning process is structured and scaffolded around curricular goals, while still allowing for inventive and authentic learning with meaningful connections made.

Inquiry learning attempts to solve problems by conceptually understanding the world through both assimilation and accommodation. It builds upon our natural curiosity of the world. As this occurs, we take in existing schema and challenge it with new information through a process of critical assessment, discussion, and through open-ended questioning that both tests our previous knowledge and evaluates against our new understandings.[26]

PROBLEM SOLVING

The goal of inquiry is to think creatively in developing solutions. The result is that when presented with a challenging problem, students sort through their mental toolbox and think flexibly about a solution or how a concept might work in a real-world context.

When students problem solve, they are tasked with deepening their thinking to overcome obstacles and find solutions to difficult or complex issues. In addition to acquiring knowledge and skills, students must also incorporate strategies to connect to life outside of the classroom.

By actively working on problems in the college classroom, students form judgments, analyze ideas, support conclusions, and learn to continually ask questions and use evaluative thinking.

By expanding students' problem-solving skills, they develop advanced dispositions to ask meaningful questions, gather and access diverse information, and challenge themselves to come up with multiple alternative possibilities on how to approach and solve a problem that they encounter in a new context, either in their personal lives or in their future careers.

These knowledge sets, skills, and dispositions are transferable across disciplines and provide a foundation for students to solve real-life problems beyond the classroom environment.[27]

CRITICAL THINKING

Because critical thinking requires a deeper level of thinking, it is also considered a form of inquiry. Critical thinking extends beyond memorized facts to using learned factual knowledge to detect patterns and then applying knowledge and skills in new and creative ways in a continual process.

Critical thinking is a learnable and necessary skill that allows students to work through difficult problems or situations using cognitive skills to deduce and make good decisions individually, creatively, and as a society.

Critical thinking strategies can be embedded throughout the curriculum so the instructor models the practice, and students are then able to replicate and receive feedback about the process.

Critical thinking requires an inquiry mindset focused on questioning. Using both simple and complex thinking strategies necessitates that an individual step back and look logically at ideas and facts that come forward and ask questions that challenge one's thinking.

The art of thinking critically will serve today's students as they become leaders of tomorrow. Imparting the ability to dissect, question, and apply information and knowledge will yield better decision makers who are able to go beyond the obvious, who see potential beyond what is immediately in front of them, and who will question objectively about a problem or content.

The ability to think critically is a higher-order skill needed to fuel innovation and creativity and is imperative for the lifelong learner. It extends beyond the recitation of facts and figures to finding ways to challenge preconceived ideas and instinctual responses. Developing the ability to think critically is a life-long pursuit where one consciously and purposely seeks out new information to continually learn, advance, and challenge one's own thinking and beliefs.

THE INQUIRY-ORIENTED CLASSROOM

In the classroom, inquiry can serve as an instructional strategy as well as a process to sequence learning, format activities, use questions, allow for open-ended research, and encourage collaborative learning.

Inquiry-based learning can meet the needs of diverse learners who have a variety of learning needs. It is personalized, student-centered, purposeful, and authentic, and offered in either synchronous or asynchronous instruction in-person or online.[28] Inquiry-oriented learning can be structured, problem-based, guided, or open-ended. In structured inquiry, the students follow the lead of the faculty member who controls the essential question or starting point for the discussion.[29]

With problem-based inquiry, students are given a real-world problem to solve, and students must apply what they learned.[30] In guided inquiry, the educator introduces topics and students formulate their own questions and develop their own resources to find answers.

Open-ended inquiry is the most free-form approach where students have the greatest freedom to explore their interests and construct their essential question, find resources and construct their learning activities, and then demonstrate learning by carrying out the project and presenting their results.[31]

Throughout the learning cycle, students explore, invent, apply, and evaluate to transform information and ideas to see relationships between what was previously learned and connect it to new information that is being learned, thus connecting facts to concepts.[32]

Within a classroom setting, instructors use different approaches to achieve the goal of learning. Inquiry-based approaches provide opportunities to enhance problem-solving skills while also developing career-ready skills and knowledge.

Using inquiry, a student works through the process of learning by exploring, asking questions, and sharing ideas being developed with others for further discussion. This moves the instructor away from a traditional teacher-centered approach toward a more student-focused and student-driven classroom.

Here the student must take ownership to develop their own thinking in more complex ways. Students are still taught and learn foundational knowledge and skills with an emphasis on developing creative thinkers and self-directed learners who ask critical questions and go beyond basic surface understanding.

Each student constructs knowledge in an individualized manner. Students come into an educational institution or classroom with their own history, past understandings, and learned experiences. A student's beliefs, attitudes, and schema, together with their learning goals, form the basis for their construction of knowledge.

In the college classroom, students move toward higher order thinking. They do this by connecting their current knowledge and skills with meaningful instruction so that they can think more creatively to solve problems and find solutions.

The idea is to cultivate skills and knowledge as well as build comprehension, communication skills, and the ability to think more critically. Curiosity and imagination help develop deeper levels of understanding. Students are connected to their learning and build cognitive skills and capacity that extends outside of the classroom.

Students take ownership of their learning and use the methods and thinking strategies practiced in class to solve problems. This helps students make connections with what they are learning and, as they are working to memorize and recall information, they are using this knowledge in new ways and in new situations to better understand how something works or fits together.

Through the cyclical process of teaching and learning, students intermingle their own world views with new theories and understandings. As the instructor incorporates planned activities, students test new information within the collective experience of the classroom by asking questions and ultimately developing new conclusions that form a reconstituted basis for their knowledge.

Naturally Curious

This inquiry-oriented learning process encourages students' natural curiosity to ask questions, gather information, and then do something meaningful with it. Critical thinking and creative engagement are at the heart of the inquiry process to promote evidence-based discussions.

The skills learned include organizational skills that support professional responsibilities such as being adaptable and flexible, as well as personal development such as collaborating and communicating with others who have diverse ideas to complete the work needed to solve complex problems.[33] The end result is a curiosity that includes the use of decision-making skills to evaluate multiple possibilities and determine the best solutions.

Within this process of inquiry and construction of knowledge, students become more aware and, as a result, actively seek out cultural and linguistic diversities. This intentionality broadens the diversity of the subject matter within the community of the classroom. Students exchange cultural ways of knowing about the topic while at the same time construct complex ways of thinking about the issue and extend their knowledge on a particular theme.

By recognizing the importance of diversity and its importance in constructing knowledge in higher education, we can engage students more directly in welcoming multiple perspectives, as well as develop skills and knowledge that will elevate advanced learning outcomes and a deeper cultural understanding.[34]

This connects to the community of practice and the need for cultural diversity to create equitable change that allows for deeper and more complex thinking. This requires having opportunities for students to become aware of multiple perspectives and experiences while also building social skills. The classroom and the entire campus should be a "safe space" to learn and grow through experience and collaboration.

An inquiry-oriented focus also provides opportunities to connect experiential learning and Dewey's learning by doing through tinkering and play in such campus spaces like makerspaces or fablabs where students come together to create, invent, and explore.

There is an active hands-on approach to learning where students take real-world materials, use their naturally curious minds, and make something of interest. These spaces are widely popular throughout education because they promote critical twenty-first-century skills in science, technology, engineering, and math (STEM).[35]

The inquiry-oriented classroom helps to deepen curiosity and learning by infusing different perspectives, ideas, and information from different backgrounds and experiences while interacting with the environment, curriculum, and one another to both challenge thinking and open the door to more creative thinking skills.

The ability to look at a problem or situation from a new perspective is a skill needed in both an interconnected world and a contemporary workspace. This creates a learner-centered classroom that focuses on outcomes, develops life learning skills, empowers students to take ownership of their learning, engages in diversity, and creates immersive learning experiences that connects to the community of inquiry where learners collaborate and engage in experiences through discourse and reflection to actively participate in making meaning in any learning space.[36]

WHOLE COLLEGE COMMUNITY OF INQUIRY

A community of inquiry strengthens relationships and connects learning experiences. The community can serve as both collaborative and social as well as cognitively independent and individually constructed.[37]

Within a community of inquiry, one can challenge previous knowledge, integrate cultural experiences, and form relationships to help elevate thinking. This cultural characteristic of learning guides our interpretations by bringing in our own background knowledge and combining it with other members knowledge to construct new knowledge.

As Vygotsky suggested, when learning in a social context a learner can build strong conceptual frameworks that interconnect ideas and approaches.[38] Working in social environments requires cognitive flexibility, a need for reflection, and opportunities to connect new meanings while also actively negotiating understandings through questioning and interaction.[39]

A community of inquiry within the university setting extends learning through a more collaborative experience. The group thinks through problems or topics to build conceptual frameworks, connecting new knowledge to existing knowledge, and always asking questions and making changes. It centers on dialog that is facilitated through this community of practice.

When adding a level of critical inquiry and a willingness to challenge thinking for change, the community looks both inward and outward to find greater significance and meaning to more complex problems.[40]

Being part of community of inquiry requires being willing to challenge both yours and others' assumptions. It requires being proactive as well as responsive to the needs of the community. For institutions of higher education, there is a continual need to critically consider new challenges that affect the institution and its many constituents both on and off the campus.

This requires the institution to make real-world connections through an experiential process that includes introspection, strategic thought, and an awareness of institutional needs and constraints while working through high level questioning and a willingness to look beyond a single viewpoint.

To practice critical thinking, strategic institutional processes and policies must engage the campus community in the process of discovery. This discovery might lead to a shift in teaching and learning models, operations, and/or policies.

In order to bring in diverse ideas, leaders collaborate with all members of the campus community to include students as well as outside entities such as other academic institutions, to include partner schools and competitors, to consider different approaches to problems or concerns.

Oftentimes, it is not the processes, procedures, or policies that are created by the administration that are important, but the construct of the institution to recognize and take creative action toward change using an inclusive process. It is through this collaborative effort that the campus community can critically work through issues and concerns using a cross cultural context and way of thinking to create more meaningful dialog and experiences across the campus.

This requires engaging a campus community toward inquiry. One in which the culture of the institution is to frame problems and find ways to solve those problems by bringing in the experiences of a diverse group of constituents with the possibilities for transformative change. This type of change can then shift behaviors of the institution, as well as its beliefs, toward a more creative mindset in thinking about higher education.

MOVING FORWARD

The main premise of a thinking curriculum is inquiry. It provokes a better understanding of the world through exploration and discovery by asking good questions, identifying quality resources and other benchmarks to analyze, synthesize, and evaluate "best" answers and ways forward.

An inquiry-oriented approach ensures that we are not just doing something for the sake of doing it. Students are not just memorizing random information to regurgitate on an exam. Administrators are not implementing copied or redundant policies with no thought as to how it is going to affect the institution. Rather, the use of inquiry is a thoughtful application of new knowledge in unique and novel ways, both for the learner as well as the institution.

As colleges and universities connect the need for career ready skills and incorporate the use of constructivist practice to ask questions and build knowledge, there is an opportunity to work toward advancement of both the institution as well as the individual student within higher education using an inquiry-oriented process.

Colleges have an opportunity to meet this moment as well as extend beyond these challenging post-pandemic times to incorporate new pedagogies and build connections within the system of the campus as well as extend relationships outside of the campus. This builds upon the premise of being a knowledge-based community and one that is also situated in constructivist principles. It resonates with an organization that is willing and eager to take on authentic and challenging problems that campuses are currently facing.

It encourages engagement with members of the campus community in an intentional process of inquiry that collectively shares and reflects on knowledge building for the campus as well as advancing the institutional processes to meet the diverse capabilities of employees and students.

Inquiry-oriented learning then is a way of asking questions to ignite innovative thinking and solve problems. It requires participants to be open and encouraging of the facilitation of productive inquiry throughout the progression of knowledge.

This process involves sharing ideas within the community and seeking out diverse ideas and experiences to create open discourse that moves beyond the surface level of the problems campuses are confronting to a deeper discussion of issues and concerns that are being encountered in today's higher education environment.

As dialog increases among diverse groups, difficult questions are asked that have the possibility to shift existing practices and processes into a new framework that advances the institution, expands the existing knowledge of the community, and supports the presence of programs, systems, and processes within the institution and its new way of thinking.

NOTES

1. John Dewey, *How We Think: A Restatement of the Relation of Reflective Thinking to the Educative Process* (Lexington, MA: D.C. Heath and Company, 1933).
2. Rebecca Barrett-Fox, "Please Do a Bad Job of Putting Your Courses Online," March 2020, https://anygoodthing.com/2020/03/12/please-do-a-bad-job-of-putting-your-courses-online/.
3. Aaron Johnson, *Online Teaching with Zoom: A Guide for Teaching and Learning with Video Conference Platforms* (Kindle, 2020).
4. John Bruner, *Acts of Meaning* (Cambridge, MA: Harvard University Press, 1990).
5. M. Gail Jones and Laura Brader-Araje, "The Impact of Constructivism on Education: Language, Discourse, and Meaning," *American Communication Journal* 5, no. 3 (2002): 1–10.
6. Emily M. Bonem, Heather Fedesco, and Angelika N. Zissimopoulos, "What You Do Is Less Important Than How you Do It: The Effects of Learning Environments on Student Outcomes," *Learning Environments Research* 23 (2020): 27–44.
7. Markie Peter and M. Folescu, "Rationalism vs. Empiricism," *The Stanford Encyclopedia of Philosophy*, Fall 2021, https://plato.stanford.edu/archives/fall2021/entries/rationalism-empiricism.
8. Gregory I. Hughes and Ayanna K. Thomas, "Retrieval Practice and Verbal Visuospatial Transfer: From Memorization to Inductive Learning," *Journal of Memory and Language* 129 (2023).
9. Susan A. Ambrose, Michael W. Bridges, Marsha C. Lovett, Michele DiPietro, and Marie K. Norman, *How Learning Works: 7 Research-Based Principles for Smart Teaching* (San Francisco, CA: Josey-Bass, 2010).
10. Wesley A Hoover, "The Practice Implications of Constructivism," *SEDL Letter* IX, no. 3 (1996).
11. Teresa Coffman, *Inquiry-Based Learning: Designing Instruction to Promote Higher Level Thinking* (Lanham, MD: Rowman & Littlefield, 2017).
12. L.S. Vygotsky, *Mind in Society: The Development of Higher Psychological Processes* (Cambridge, MA: Harvard University Press, 1978).
13. Marcy P. Driscoll and Kerry J. Burner, *Psychology of Learning for Instruction* (Needham Heights, MA: Allyn & Bacon, 2000).
14. Jean Piaget, *The Psychology of the Child* (New York: Basic Books, 1972).
15. Rachel Spronken-Smith, "Experiencing the Process of Knowledge Creation: The Nature and Use of Inquiry-Based Learning in Higher Education," *International Colloquium on Practices for Academic Inquiry University of Otago* (2012): 1–17.
16. S.O. Bada and Steve Olusegun, "Constructivism Learning Theory: A Paradigm for Teaching and Learning," *Journal of Research & Method in Education* 5, no. 6 (2015): 66–70.
17. Chih-Hsiung Tu and Michael Corry, "Building Active Online Interaction Via a Collaborative Learning Community," *Computers in the Schools* 20, no. 3 (2003): 51–59.

18. M. Suzanne Donovan, John D. Bransford, and James W. Pellegrino, *How People Learn: Brain, Mind, Experience, and School* (Washington, DC: The National Academies Press, 2000).

19. Emery Schubert, "Creativity Is Optimal Novelty and Maximum Positive Affect: A New Definition Based on the Spreading Activation Model," *Front Neuroscience* (2021). 15:612379.

20. Gordon Vessels, "The Creative Process: An Open-Systems Conceptualization," *Journal of Creative Behavior* 16 (1982): 185–96.

21. Spencer Harrison, Elizabeth D. Rouse, Colin M. Fisher, and Teresa M. Amabile, "The Turn Toward Creative Work," *Academy of Management Collections* 1, no. 1 (2022): 1–15.

22. Joy P. Guilford, "Creativity: Yesterday, Today and Tomorrow," *The Journal of Creative Behavior* 1, no. 1 (1967): 3–14.

23. Jon Kolko, *Wicked Problems: Problems Worth Solving: A Handbook and a Call to Action* (Austin TX: Austin Center for Design, 2012).

24. Stephen P. Robbins and Timothy A. Judge, *Organizational Behavior* (Upper Saddle River, NJ: Pearson, 2019).

25. Douglas Thomas and John Seely Brown, "A New Culture of Learning: Cultivating the Imagination for a World of Constant Change" (self-published, CreateSpace, 2011).

26. Jacqueline Grennon Brooks and Martin G. Brooks, *In Search of Understanding: The Case for Constructivist Classrooms* (Alexandria, VA: American Society for Curriculum Development, 1999).

27. Dewey, *How We Think*.

28. Yong Zhao and Jim Watterston, "The Changes We Need: Education Post COVID-19," *Journal of Educational Change* 22 (2021): 3–12.

29. Trevor MacKenzie, "Bringing Inquiry-Based Learning into Your Class," Edutopia, December 1, 2016, https://www.edutopia.org/article/bringing-inquiry-based-learning-into-your-class-trevor-mackenzie.

30. "What Is Inquiry-Based Learning? Types, Benefits, Examples," *SplashLearn*, February 9, 2023, https://www.splashlearn.com/blog/what-is-inquiry-based-learning-a-complete-overview/.

31. Andrew Bauld, "What Is Inquiry-Based Learning?" Rethink Together, February 14, 2022, https://xqsuperschool.org/rethinktogether/what-is-inquiry-based-learning-ibl/.

32. Walter L. Bateman, *Open to Question: The Art of Teaching and Learning by Inquiry* (San Francisco: Jossey-Bass, 1990).

33. "Top 11 Skills Employers Look for in Job Candidates," Indeed, October 27, 2022, https://www.indeed.com/career-advice/resumes-cover-letters/skills-employers-look-for.

34. Josh Moody, "Diversity in College and Why It Matters," *U.S. News Education*, March 31, 2020, https://www.usnews.com/education/best-colleges/articles/diversity-in-college-and-why-it-matters.

35. "What Is a Makerspace?" 2022, https://www.makerspaces.com/what-is-a-makerspace/.

36. Sheri Conklin and Amy Garrett Dikkers, "Instructor Social Presence and Connectedness in a Quick Shift from Face-To-Face to Online Instruction," *Online Learning* 25, no. 1 (2021).

37. Norman D. Vaughan, Martha Cleveland-Innes, and D. Randy Garrison, *Teaching in Blended Learning Environments: Creating and Sustaining Communities of Inquiry* (Edmonton, AB: AU Press, Athabasca University, 2013).

38. Luis C. Moll, *Vygotsky and Education: Instructional Implications and Applications of Sociohistorical Psychology* (Cambridge, MA: Cambridge University Press, 1990).

39. Ambrose et al., *How Learning Works*, 2010.

40. Becky Dyer and T. Löytönen, "Engaging Dialogue: Co-Creating Communities of Collaborative Inquiry," *Research in Dance Education* 13, no. 1 (2011): 121–47.

Chapter Eight

Managing in the Post-Pandemic Era

You must do things you think you cannot do.

—Eleanor Roosevelt, *You Learn by Living*

The pandemic has served as a catalyst paradoxically for *both* stability and innovation. This dichotomy is unsettling but true. While everyone craves a return to "normal," no institution can—or wants to—stand still. The pre-pandemic university is now a memory as are many of the needed leadership actions that were undertaken during the COVID-19 crisis. Presently, a focus toward strategic planning initiatives based on current circumstances is needed.

Institutions have gathered copious amounts of data and information to support critical decisions moving forward. These internal reference points are analyzed and scrutinized to determine next steps. A review and monitoring of the external environment is also needed. We have seen unprecedented changes both internally and externally as colleges have navigated through the pandemic.

As these transformations become more well-defined over time, it is critical to ensure that the necessary knowledge factors are in place so information—whether it is tacit or explicit—is absorbed transparently and organizationally so it is not leaving the institution unnecessarily.

In light of the Great Resignation and the employment changes we are presently seeing across academia, retaining talent throughout the organization is the new imperative for the institution and the students it serves.[1] It will be difficult, if not impossible, to retrieve knowledge once key knowledge centers are dismantled and/or college personnel exit the organization.[2]

In the current global landscape of higher education, colleges and universities are knowledge-driven institutions. Global competition for students is now commonplace and new technologies to deliver instruction or support internal processes are more available across the institution.

The ability for the university to innovate has always been a strategic advantage and source of strength. Now, more than ever before, the ability of higher education to function as an agile, flexible, and responsive institution has never been more needed.[3]

As educational institutions evolve and seek to innovate and transform to meet the challenges of today's rapidly changing landscape, institutional leadership strives to unify critical understanding and implement strategic initiatives that underscore and cement the institution's purpose and reason for being.[4] Solid management principles can be used for this process.

Management is enveloped within four primary areas to include planning, leading, organizing, and controlling. Management's goal is to ensure order and stability in trying to fulfill the institution's promise. Leadership, on the other hand, strives to encourage change and transformation so that organizational processes are improved, and the vision achieved.

An understanding of management principles will solidify the relationship needed in an organization between effective management and future-driven leadership for educational institutions going forward. Key aspects of planning, organizing, leading, and controlling are discussed below and leadership is explored more deeply in the next chapter.

PLANNING

The planning function is by far the most popular aspect of management. Organizations continually seek ways to navigate a clear path forward. Planning involves organizing departments and their functions to identify tasks and processes needed to meet short-term objectives and achieve the longer-term goals of the institution. The planning process is a critical component for all organizations and applies to a start-up institution or a large university and everything else in between.

Whether a large state-run university, a small community college in a rural part of the Midwest, or a private college in the Northeast, the management skills and leadership acumen needed to navigate through the current climate—be it political, economic, sociocultural, technological, legal, or environmental—all starts with having clear goals and the flexibility to determine what is needed at the moment to ensure that the educational institution is able to reach its desired aim.

Different levels of planning are necessary depending on the level within the organization. For example, operational planning is generally completed by first-level managers or department chairs with staffing courses, semester schedules, and resource needs to complete departmental level projects.

Tactical planning is done at the mid or college level in terms of specific objectives as designated by the institution's strategic plan. These tend to have a more short-term focus, for example, a year or less, such as setting an annual budget.

Strategic planning is performed at the highest levels of the institution in terms of broad, long-range goals, for example, more than a year, that are communicated through the strategic plan. It is the strategic plan that is broadly published and shared with all stakeholders both internal and external to the college community. Contingency planning is also important in terms of backup plans and risk management procedures as witnessed most recently with the pandemic.

Vision

Ultimately the organization's true vision comes from those at the top of the organizational chart. This then is translated down the organizational structure and throughout the organization. It is also shared externally throughout the community.

The vision for the institution always comes from leadership or top managers. The leadership team must have a vision and be able to express that vision to the rest of the organization as well as to outside stakeholders. Without a vision, the institution is like a boat with no rudder.

First and foremost, it is incumbent among the leadership team to ensure that the institution's vision aligns with the current external environment and with the university's organizational capabilities. The vision should demonstrate to the outside world why it exists. It defines not just a vision for the college or university at present, but where top management envisions the institution going into the future.

Personal leadership also factors in with regard to a vision for the future and how, for example, the college president sees the organization "becoming." In consultation with the board of trustees and other senior managers, the institution's vision is formed. In true shared governance, other parts of the college community should also weigh in on the most appropriate vision for the institution in keeping with common traditions and current times.

Skilled leaders do not react to events but are guided by the vision of the institution. They work in collaboration with a strong leadership team that can manage through a crisis, such as the pandemic. Following an emergency, they are able to learn from the experience, adjust, and prepare for the next crisis.[5]

Mission

The institution's vision is articulated and formalized into a mission statement. The mission statement should succinctly state the organization's fundamental purpose. It must be truthful. In other words, the mission statement reflects the values to guide employees' actions and the initiatives of the organization.[6] If these values are not upheld, the organization loses its direction.

Those integral to the university, that is, students, faculty, staff, and the community, see right through a mission statement if it is not accurate or tells falsehoods. The result will be people—internal or external—pulling away from the organization and not trusting it to recognize their best interests or to lead in times of crisis.

The vision for the organization and its mission should be updated following change, such as the pandemic. Neither the institution's vision nor its mission is set in stone. These statements should be revisited, challenged, and updated as circumstances warrant. A well-constructed vision and mission will bind the organization together into a more coordinated and collective culture.[7]

Goals and Objectives

Following the establishment of the vision and mission statement, institutional goals and objectives are defined. Goals are broad, long-term aims, while objectives are shorter-term with more specific details on how achieving the objectives will meet the larger term goals.

For example, a goal for many higher educational institutions is to increase enrollments. An objective in this scenario might be to work with local K–12 schools to offer dual enrollment options to students with high school recruiting events planned.[8] Goals and objectives flow from the vision and mission, so when these are updated, the corresponding goals and objectives must likewise be reworked and reintroduced.

Strategic Planning Tools

There are many popular planning tools that can be used in an organization's planning process. One popular and straight forward tool is the SWOT analysis as shown in figure 8.1. Examining the institution's *strengths*, *weaknesses*, *opportunities*, and *threats*, the SWOT explores the college's internal strengths and weaknesses, and investigates its external opportunities and threats.

While a SWOT analysis can be conducted by senior-level leadership, its results and information gathered should not stop there. Management's realization of the results of this important tool involves conducting a SWOT analysis with as many of its stakeholders as possible, both internal to the institution and outside of the university as well.[9] A college president will have a very different interpretation of the institution's strengths when presiding over a graduation ceremony, for example, then a new student who has trouble navigating the online semester schedule.

Internal	S	Strengths
	W	Weaknesses
External	O	Opportunities
	T	Threats

Figure 8.1. SWOT Analysis

In addition to garnering input from a variety of stakeholders, the SWOT analysis should also be done fairly frequently if the organization is changing quite substantially and dramatically as we have seen during and since the pandemic. In this current hyper-changing climate, at least every two years would be the recommendation until the environment stabilizes. When the institution is operating in relatively stable times, reevaluating the SWOT analysis every three to four years is a satisfactory goal.

The PESTLE analysis illustrated in figure 8.2 is another popular planning tool used to examine the external environment by exploring the *political, economic, social, technological, legal,* and *environmental* aspects currently impacting the educational institution.[10] The PESTLE analysis reinforces the opportunities and threats gleaned from the SWOT analysis and can serve as an effective tool for determining strategic goals as related to the external environment.

ORGANIZING

The second aspect of the management process focuses on the institution's organizational structure. How is the institution set up? Is it a line-and-staff structure, matrix, or does it operate using cross functional self-managed teams? For larger institutions, the university may have a combination of structures depending on the college or department. For smaller colleges, a homogeneous structure may be most appropriate.

Traditionally within education, institutions have tended to revolve around functional silos. This is mainly a hierarchical structure with a strong chain of command. It may also tend toward a bureaucratic structure depending on the institution's size and whether it is public or private.

P	Political
E	Economic
S	Social
T	Technological
L	Legal
E	Environmental

Figure 8.2. PESTLE Analysis

Line-and-Staff Structure

Historically in higher education there has existed a strong edifice and delineation between faculty and administration, which coincides somewhat with the line-and-staff organizational model.

Faculty are the line personnel based on their teaching interactions with students given that education is the main organizational mission. Some administrators who are directly student-facing are also part of the line structure such that they advise or work with students directly.

Administrators who assist the organization in meeting goals through efforts such as information technology, finance, human resources, marketing, and legal relations with little to no student contact or interactions would be part of the staff structure. Whether an employee is line or staff, each are equally important to the successful running of the institution. A simplified organizational chart is shown in figure 8.3.

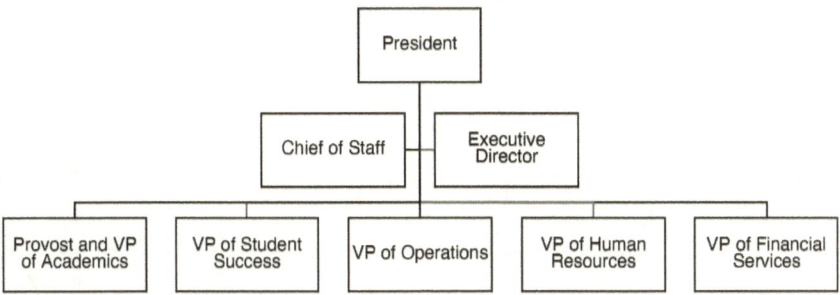

Figure 8.3. Sample Organizational Chart

Matrix Organizations

To provide greater flexibility and faster implementation of ideas, educational institutions today tend to be matrix organizations. Here we see the traditional line-and-staff structure as described above with functional responsibilities. Added in are additional committees and workgroups set up and coming together from different parts of the organization to collaborate short- or long-term on projects and university processes critical to the functioning of the institution.

As illustrated in figure 8.4, an employee may be part of the "line" or "staff" function, but then additionally—and temporarily—brought over to work on a hiring committee, for example. Once the hiring is complete, the committee disbands. Participatory governance is another example of employees from different departments joining together to make decisions on educational matters affecting the institution.[11]

Various employees are involved in different committees and projects in a matrix style environment. When a community or governance issue is solved or a project such as reaccreditation completed, employees return to their functional areas in the line-and-staff structure. Frequently, college employees are involved in multiple projects away from and in addition to their line or staff responsibilities.

The matrix organizational structure has several advantages that make it ideal for higher education. These include the following:

- Flexibility in placing faculty and staff into different temporary projects
- Institutional employees increase interorganizational collaboration and teamwork through participation in varied activities
- More creative solutions to organizational opportunities, issues, and problems can be developed with diverse groups
- The institution's resources can be used more efficiently because only a select group of people are coming together for a limited period to solve a specific issue or create a particular project[12]

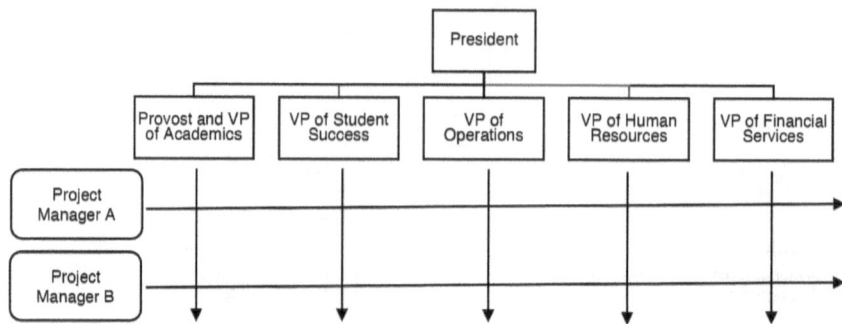

Figure 8.4. Sample Matrix Organization

Cross-Functional Self-Managed Teams

The educational institution of the future may advance even beyond the more traditional line-and-staff approach and move ahead of the matrix style organization by instituting a more innovative organizational structure known as cross-functional self-managed teams. This type of structure works best in organizations that are changing rapidly and need to be agile.[13]

A cross-functional self-managed team approach means that employees are hired for specific skills (e.g., a professor of linguistics or a professor of accounting). Staff are similarly brought on board for the profession they are skilled in such as marketing, accounting, or human resources.

As illustrated in figure 8.5, teams are then formed around specific issues needed to run the organization. Employees throughout the educational institution work together in teams both long-term and shorter-term depending on the project. They do not return to a line-and-staff role at the conclusion of a project simply because a line-and-staff department does not exist. Every task is decided in teams, and when one project is concluded, the group will disband, and personnel will then move to another team with a new issue, problem, or opportunity.

Even more innovative is involving not just internal employees from throughout the institution, but additionally bringing in external stakeholders who include students, community members, political constituencies, and suppliers to offer additional insight or support on a given issue.

The true emphasis of innovation in this structure means that groups are formed beyond institutional confines. Transparency and networking are critical to higher education thriving in the years to come. By allowing internal and external stakeholders to work together on common objectives it advances the institution and the community it serves.[14]

Internally, the most innovative institutions resist adding bureaucratic layers to the organization and shy away from becoming mechanistic and rigid. This can be difficult for colleges and universities that are heavily state supported given the bureaucratic nature of state governments.

Rather than being mechanistic, those institutions that are more organically structured have less formalization and tend to be more flexible and adaptive. Employees work across organizational functions or "silos." Innovation is more porous and free flowing across the enterprise when the institution has more communication across departmental lines.

Given the continued need for change and flexibility within education amid all the transformations we have witnessed throughout the most recent past, the future of education appears to only be accelerating. Institutions using cross-functional teams or a matrix structure to facilitate interactions tend to see greater innovative performance such that fewer barriers separate employees internally. The more permeable the internal structure, the more innovative the results.

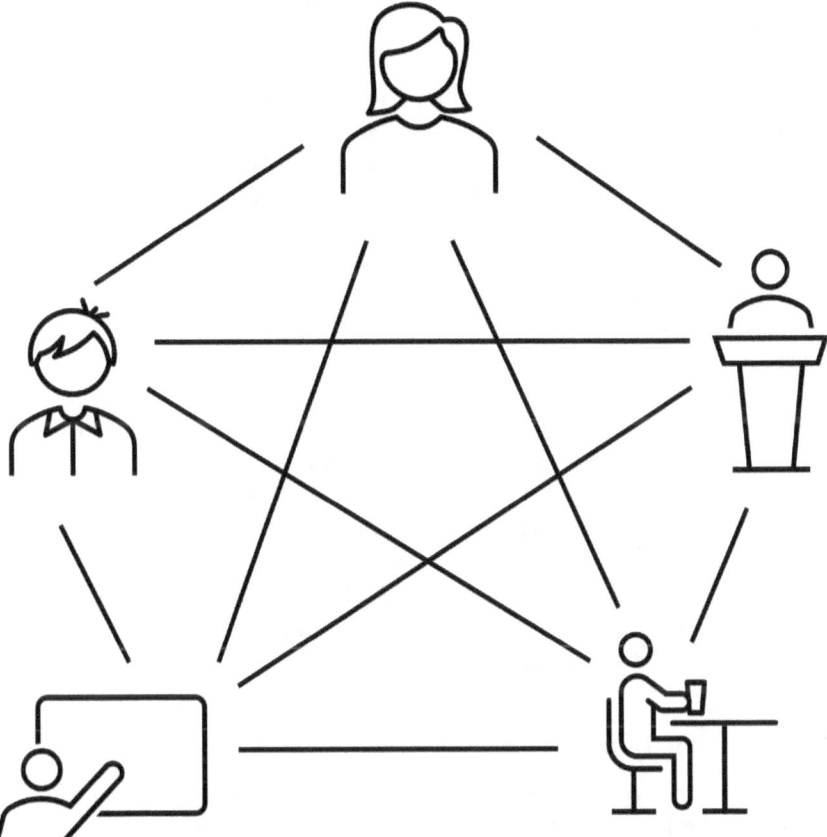

Figure 8.5. Sample Cross-Functional Self-Managed Team

This presents to the community a management team and leadership that is open and flexible as well as transparent, welcoming social interaction, and incorporating dialog from both inside and outside the campus.

LEADING

The leading function as mentioned above establishes the vision for the institution, and it works to implement the goals and objectives established in the planning process through empowering employees, using knowledge management, and other current age management practices.

Attracting, motivating, and retaining a quality workforce at all levels of the institution is key to maintaining a world-class educational organization in today's fast-changing environment. Innovative leaders reward cross-functional, cross-hierarchical, cross-cultural, and cross-technological exchanges of information and knowledge because they realize the value of sharing and collaborating across the institution.

One aspect of effective leadership is ensuring that your employees share your institution's vision and that they are on board in helping to achieve it.[15] Education is a sharing profession, therefore employees drawn to the educational environment tend to be very giving and passionate about helping others.

As an organizational leader, it is important to service this passion for the greater good of both the institution and the students served. Encouraging people to question and engage in understanding the "why" is an important step toward a deeper conversation regarding why the institution exists and where it should lead.

Presently, post-pandemic, we are seeing resignations and retirements from employees across the board and higher education is no exception. Current job openings are numerous for staff, faculty, and institutional leadership. Leadership has been particularly hard hit with multiple openings in leadership positions such as provost, dean, and department chairs.[16]

As these upper-level positions turn over with new personnel, the vision will shift and change as people come and go. Additionally, if the community or external environment in which the institution operates is changing, the vision will need to be adapted and updated as well.

Organizational Culture

The culture that exists within the institution is extremely important to determining the level of innovative success.[17] Universities are truly about the people who work and study in them.[18] Establishing an organizational culture that is open to experimentation and is not afraid of failure sends a strong signal up-and-down the organizational chart.

Valuing autonomy, offering flexible workspaces, and giving employees control over their schedules as much as possible is an important step in ensuring that employees feel heard and as though college leadership has their best interests at heart. This contributes to an entrepreneurial mindset, where employees are comfortable taking the initiative and know their input will be valued.

Establishing strong and robust mentor systems for staff, faculty, and students sends a strong message about commitment to individual success and long-term sustainability of the institution. It creates a community of practice that helps employees be flexible and adaptive in a collective atmosphere of caring, respect, and trust. It also establishes resilient networking ties that can be strengthened throughout—and even beyond—someone's tenure at the institution.

Avoiding Burnout

Education is a challenging profession. One that can be both draining and strenuous. Those in higher education can attest that the climate of instruction and the institutions themselves have been upended since early 2020 at the start of the COVID-19 pandemic.

Mental health has received well-deserved attention and the phrase "quiet quitting" is now being applied within education as a way for educators to set boundaries and preserve their mental health.[19] Quiet quitting or said in a more positive manner—finding work life balance—is a way to help manage mental health challenges and navigate personal and professional responsibilities so that one can hold a sense of personal well-being while also honoring professional expectations.

Working in higher education during the past several years has been difficult due to the pandemic and has impacted everyone in physical and emotional ways. This has resulted in greater burnout, brought on by fatigue and frustration, resulting in employees leaving academia and faculty leaving the teaching profession.[20]

"Givers" or those who consistently and selflessly put others first are often most prone to burnout. Caution must be taken not to overload and help everyone with every request without boundaries. Despite best intentions, a selfless educator, one who consistently drains their own resources, time, and energy, can become exhausted using this approach.[21]

Self-care and empowerment of one's own life and decisions are imperative to restoring a sense of personal and professional balance. Restorative opportunities to treat burnout are different depending on its cause and the symptoms exhibited.[22] It is incumbent upon the leadership within an organization to monitor its culture and support employee mental health throughout the workplace.[23]

Many organizations outside of education are actively trying to manage work life balance and ensure that their employees are not tapped out. Mozilla, for example, which produces the Firefox Web browser, shuts down the company for "Wellness Week" and LinkedIn also closed its doors to allow its employees to recharge.[24]

Setting boundaries in the world of 24/7 higher education demands has become paramount.[25] For faculty and staff that are staying in their jobs, many are seeking ways to actively engage in collaboration with colleagues across campus for support and community.

Educators are sharing best practices within their professional communities to feel more emotionally present in the classroom and for the university.[26] Within the classroom, faculty are working to change their teaching practice such as incorporating more introspective methods, building community, facilitating discussion, and advancing equity and inclusion into their pedagogy. Additionally, they are finding ways to decompress from teaching and research responsibilities once they have left the campus, while still meeting the standards expected.[27]

College administration is working with employees to discuss workloads and flexible schedules to provide more support during the pandemic and now post-pandemic. While educational leadership recognizes the importance of an engaged and committed workforce, institutional support has been varied across campuses as colleges try to navigate next steps in teaching and learning.[28]

Most college leadership is aware of the potential for burnout and overwork on behalf of faculty and staff. Finding ways to develop a more positive work culture that involves building relationships and creative collaborations across campus—without creating more work—is the new order of the day for some of the most progressive and thoughtful organizations.

Learning Organization

A focused vision and strategy for meeting next-generational needs, coupled with an organizational culture and internal processes in the institution that reward risk-taking and innovative practices are now center point for the post-pandemic educational institution.[29]

The management style and leadership capabilities within higher education must mirror those of the "learning organization," a term originally coined by Peter Senge.[30] This is an institution where employees feel supported to change, adapt, and grow. The process of rejuvenation is continual and commonplace, not just in times of crisis.

This innovative strategy, combined with a forward-looking strategic plan, yields an institutional culture of employees—faculty and staff—who are excited about change and experimentation—both throughout the college or university's administrative units as well as in teaching and learning.

Being open to new experiences and opportunities allows the institution to experiment and try something new. Institutional-wide support encourages everyone to provide diverse input and share ideas. This attitude will be apparent to students as well throughout the institution, which will result in even greater innovation and new ideas.

True learning organizations facilitate an inquisitive mindset that allows the institution to continue to grow and adapt. The external environment that revolves around the college or university demands an organizational culture of adaptability and flexibility, and given today's times, one that is open to ambiguity. This can be disconcerting from a leadership and management stance, but when learning and a growth mindset are part of the college's culture, there is an aptitude for novelty and openness to change.

Collaborative organizations that promote learning and encourage experimentation tend to be more successful than those who rely on using competition to motivate employees or students. A competitive mindset reduces knowledge sharing and results in reduced cooperation and collaboration.[31]

Similarly, it is necessary to try and manage change efforts. Too much change can create chaos and confusion, which results in frustration and lack of a sense of control. Positioning the organization in a proactive rather than reactive stance can yield greater results with learning and creating something new.

When an institution is constantly in a reactive mode, such as with the pulls-and-pushes of the pandemic, the result is that managers and employees are continuously trying to problem solve from one issue to the next. It is hard for the organization to be innovative and focus on improving and creating a learning organization when employees are always "putting out fires."[32]

CONTROLLING

This is the fourth management function that often receives the least amount of attention. It is just as critical as the other three. Once an institution has completed its planning, designed its organizational structure, and created effective leadership, then the final step in the management process is to determine if the college did what it intended.

Using the controlling function of management, clear standards and measurement tools are put in place so the institution can determine if the goals and objectives of the organization were achieved, and if not, what corrective actions need to be applied.

The control process provides the communication and feedback regarding any necessary adjustments needed in the planning process or the management continuum as impacted by internal changes or external events that may have taken place.

As shown in figure 8.6, the control process is a five-step continual feedback loop that

- starts with establishing clear standards,
- monitors and records performance and results,
- compares results achieved against previously set standards,
- communicates the results and as needed,
- takes corrective action to support new information or data.[33]

Within education, the college's institutional research department does much of the data and statistical analysis in the monitoring and recording process. They then communicate the data and information both internally to needed departments as well as externally to accreditation bodies and local, state, and federal agencies.

MOVING FORWARD

Utilizing solid management practices ensures that the institution remains responsive to its employees, students, and the community. Applying the four functions of management—planning, organizing, leading, and controlling—

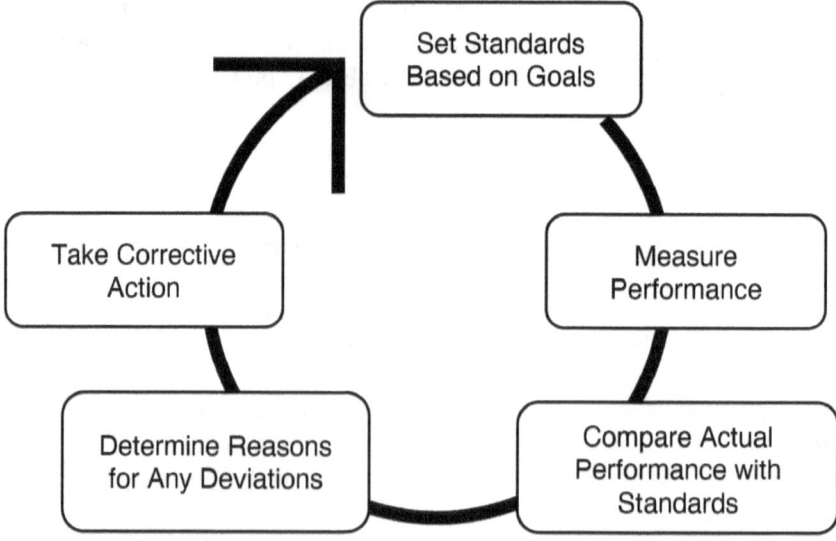

Figure 8.6. The Control Process

to the educational institution is useful when developing the strategic plan and formulating next steps.

It is critical that the organizational structure connects to the strategic plan and leading an institution post-pandemic. This chapter considered the need to reshape an organization's culture where managers at all levels demonstrate through action a need to take risks and dream big to create more agility in systems and processes moving forward so the institution can be its most dynamic and responsive.

With this mindset, there is a need for the institution to function as a learning organization and to be open and willing to connect to new information as it builds on previous knowledge and experiences.[34] This approach centers around higher education's mission to be a knowledge creator while also engaging in knowledge dissemination.

NOTES

1. Carrie Hawes and Samara Reynolds, "Radical Retention: How Higher Education Can Rise to the Challenges of the Great Resignation and Beyond," National Association of Colleges and Employers, August 1, 2022, https://www.naceweb.org/career-development/best-practices/radical-retention-how-higher-education-can-rise-to-the-challenges-of-the-great-resignation-and-beyond/.

2. Chun Wei Choo, *The Management of Learning: Organizations as Knowledge-Creating Enterprises* (Oxford Academic, 2005), 127–98.

3. Chun Wei Choo, *The Management of Learning*.

4. Linda L. Baer, Ann Hill Duin, and Judith A. Ramaley, "Smart Change," *Planning for Higher Education* 36, no. 2 (2008): 5–16.

5. Mark W. Johnson and Josh Suskewicz, "Leaders, Do You Have a Clear Vision for the Post-Crisis Future?" *Harvard Business Review,* April 17, 2020, https://hbr.org/2020/04/leaders-do-you-have-a-clear-vision-for-the-post-crisis-future.

6. Julián D. Cortés, Liliana Rivera, and Katerina Bohle Carbonelld, "Mission Statements in Universities: Readability and Performance," *European Research on Management and Business Economics* 28, no. 2 (2022).

7. John Marshall and M. Adamic, "The Story Is the Message: Shaping Corporate Culture," *Journal of Business Strategy* 31 (2010): 18–23.

8. "Dual Enrollment Research: A Comprehensive Review," Southern Regional Education Board, June 2020, https://www.sreb.org/sites/main/files/file-attachments/dual_enrollment_2020.pdf.

9. Jiju Antony, "A SWOT Anaysis on Six Sigma: Some Perspectives from Leading Academic and Practitioners," *International Journal of Productivity and Performance Management* 61, no. 6: (2012).

10. "What is the PESTLE Analysis? An Important Business Analysis Tool," Pestle Analysis, January 1, 2023, https://pestleanalysis.com/what-is-pestle-analysis/.

11. Sidney Hirsch and Lawrence C. Shulman, "Participatory Governance: A Model for Shared Decision Making," *Social Work in Health Care* 1, no. 4 (1976): 433–46.

12. William Nickels, Jim McHugh, and Susan McHugh, *Understanding Business* (New York: McGraw-Hill, 2015).

13. Stephanie Jones and Dave Cass, "Agile Leadership: Eight Steps to Becoming an Agile Team Leader," *Effective Executive* 24, no. 1 (2022): 7–12.

14. Chris James, Michael Connolly, and Melissa Hawkins, "Reconceptualizing and Redefining Educational Leadership Practice, *Theory and Practice* 23, no. 5: (2019): 618–35.

15. Theodore M. Hesburgh, "The Presidency: A Personalist Manifesto," 59th Annual Meeting of the American Council on Education, New Orleans, Louisiana, October 7, 1976, https://archives.nd.edu/Hesburgh/CPHS142-09-07.pdf.

16. Melissa Fuesting, Sarah Nadel-Hawhthorn, Anthony Schmidt, and Jacqueline Bischsel, "Professionals in Higher Education Annual Report: Key Findings, Trends, and Comprehensive Tables for the 2020–21 Academic Year Overview," College and University Professional Association for Human Resources, 2021.

17. Benn Lawson and Danny Samson, "Developing Innovation Capability in Organizations: A Dynamic Capabilities Approach," *International Journal of Innovation Management* 5 (2001): 377–400.

18. Alasdair Blair and Sarah Jones, "University Leaders Need to Demonstrate an Adaptive Mindset," *The Times Higher Education,* September 8, 2021, https://www.timeshighereducation.com/campus/university-leaders-need-demonstrate-adaptive-mindset.

19. Leah Jackson and Kelly A. Cherwin, "Could 'Quiet Quitting' Spell Trouble for Higher Ed?" Higher Ed Jobs, October 4, 2022, https://www.higheredjobs.com/Articles/articleDisplay.cfm?ID=3204.

20. Jacqueline Bichsel, Melissa Fuesting, Jennifer Schneider, and Diana Tubbs, "The CUPA-HR 2022 Higher Education Employee Retention Survey: Initial Results," College and University Professional Association for Human Resources, July 2022, https://www.cupahr.org/surveys/research-briefs/higher-ed-employee-retention-survey-findings-july-2022/.

21. Adam Grant and Reb Rebele, "Beat Generosity Burnout," *Harvard Business Review*, January 23, 2017, https://hbr.org/2017/01/beat-generosity-burnout.

22. Yu Tse Heng and Kira Schabram, "Your Burnout Is Unique. Your Recovery Will Be, Too," *Harvard Business Review*, April 12, 2021, https://hbr.org/2021/04/your-burnout-is-unique-your-recovery-will-be-too.

23. Ashley Wu, Enid Chung Roemer, Karen B. Kent, David W. Ballard, and Ron Z. Goetzel, "Organizational Best Practices Supporting Mental Health in the Workplace," *Journal of Occupational and Environmental Medicine* 63, no. 12 (2021).

24. Soo Youn, "America's Workers Are Exhausted and Burned Out—and Some Employers Are Taking Notice," *The Washington Post*, June 29, 2021, https://www.washingtonpost.com/business/2021/06/28/employee-burnout-corporate-america/.

25. Paul Musgrave, "The Season of Our Professional Discontent," *The Chronicle of Higher Education*, June 9, 2022, https://www.chronicle.com/article/the-season-of-our-professorial-discontent.

26. Bonni Stachowiak, "Teaching in Higher Ed" *Podcast*, 2023, https://teachinginhighered.com/episodes/.

27. Adam Grant, "Burnout Isn't Just in Your Head. It's in Your Circumstances," *The New York Times,* March 19, 2020, https://www.nytimes.com/2020/03/19/smarter-living/coronavirus-emotional-support.html.

28. Stephanie Saul, "At N.Y.U., Students Were Failing Organic Chemistry. Who Was to Blame?" *The New York Times,* October 3, 2022, https://www.nytimes.com/2022/10/03/us/nyu-organic-chemistry-petition.html.

29. Simon L. Dolan, Mario Raich, Anat Garti, and Avishai Landau, "The COVID-19 Crisis as an Opportunity for Introspection: A Multi-Level Reflection on Values, Needs, Trust and Leadership in the Future," *The European Business Review*, August 6, 2020, https://www.europeanbusinessreview.com/the-covid-19-crisis-as-an-opportunity-for-introspection/.

30. David A. Garvin, "Building a Learning Organization," *Harvard Business Review,* July-August, 1993, https://hbr.org/1993/07/building-a-learning-organization.

31. Stephen P. Robbins and Timothy A. Judge, *Organizational Behavior* (Upper Saddle River, NJ: Pearson, 2018).

32. Robbins and Judge, *Organizational Behavior*.

33. Nickels, McHugh, and McHugh, *Understanding Business*.

34. Garvin, "Building a Learning Organization."

Chapter Nine

Leading toward Change

Education is the most powerful weapon which you can use to change the world.

—Nelson Mandela

A leader meets the needs of the times. They move the institution forward, even when a global health crisis surfaces. Prior to the COVID-19 pandemic and before the rapid transition to remote learning, many educational institutions were struggling with low enrollments combined with rising costs and shrinking budgets.

Since the pandemic, we have seen some colleges close their doors.[1] Others are considering merging to survive.[2] And some aptly positioned institutions have found ways to evolve—and thrive—in this new landscape.[3] Today, these transitions continue. Over the past decade, leadership in higher education pre-, during, and post-COVID has been accentuated by one continual mantra—*change*. And this change is taking many different forms.

The change efforts, whether focused on online teaching, remote work, mental health, college affordability, student enrollment, retention, diversity and equity, not to mention the changing political, economic, social, and technological landscapes, as well as the pandemic-related adjustments have all placed a tremendous amount of strain on academic leadership as well as the institution itself.

There is a new normal that governing boards and presidents of colleges and universities must navigate as they lead higher education into the next era while the continued day-to-day nuances of running an educational institution march on.

EDUCATIONAL LEADERSHIP

Educational leaders who oversee the academic and administrative operations of their respective institutions are called to meet this era. Throughout the pandemic crisis, college presidents and higher education leadership understandably struggled to respond timely and consistently in ways that were student, employee, and community focused while balancing the demands of state, federal, and their own institutional boards to retain critical institutional needs and services and at the same time, maintain financial solvency.[4] It was *not* an easy time.

As institutions move past the pandemic, effective leadership requires an understanding of conceptual skills and the umbrella-level knowledge and expertise to govern the inner workings of the organization. This includes big picture insight regarding the institution as a whole and an understanding of how the different parts fit together.

A college's leadership team must use the same foundational skills that higher education is teaching its students, for example, synthesizing, listening, interpreting, evaluating, communicating, and applying to ensure that the institution's vision and values are carried out, the strategic plan implemented, and that the university remains forward-thinking.[5]

The college president uses a 360-degree leadership approach that leads downward into the institution, as well as upward with governing boards, state governors, business leaders, and alumni. There is a continual emphasis on being collaborative as the president works with the administration and faculty to advance the college's strategic plan in keeping with the vision and purpose of the institution.[6]

Collaboration is a core necessity of an effective leader. It requires coalescing faculty and staff to partner with one another as they work on programs and other projects. Collaborative leadership is the ability of a leader to both inspire and bring together diverse stakeholders both on and off campus while also working through challenging problems.

This comprehensive leadership requires a college president to be open and adaptable and to listen carefully and actively so that there is clear communication across the university. This allows the institution to be accepting of change, willing to innovate and explore, able to effectively manage threats and advance opportunities so that it remains viable and relevant.

This leadership style requires a continual sense of intellectual curiosity, one that is comfortable promoting change, and willing to test the status quo to advance and improve the institution to meet current and future challenges.[7] Having a leadership team focused on a growth mindset allows the institution to acknowledge that challenges exist and then support a flexible approach in finding solutions.

Changing Leadership Dimensions

As college leadership adjusts to the new normal, there is now more than ever a need for academic leadership to navigate an institution that is agile, resourceful, adaptive, and innovative.[8]

Today's leadership necessitates an all-encompassing focus along with a transformational outlook to meet the current challenges facing college campuses. It starts with identifying what is working and what can be improved, thereby creating tactical, strategic, and progressive paths forward for the institution.[9]

Leadership's role is one of compassion and empathy to support the well-being of the campus and at the same time work with all constituents to find ways to create a shared and engaged purpose throughout the institution that is sustainable and relevant.[10]

Faculty and staff may feel alienated and disengaged as the pandemic recedes and pressures of campus life reemerge.[11] These feelings did not start with the pandemic but have been exacerbated by it.[12]

As the administration recognizes internal issues and problems and continually tries to find workable and equitable solutions, discussions must be facilitated with those that are feeling disengaged or displaced.[13] Ignoring these problems is not an option. To build a strong, resilient culture requires leadership to listen and respond effectively.

TRANSFORMATIONAL CHANGE

Our best leaders embrace change efforts that support transformation of processes and activities and engage with change forerunners throughout the organization to plant the seed of commitment to change and the positive evolution of the organization. Leaders reinforce invention, allocate resources to support change efforts, and positively express the need for adjustments such that it funnels its way throughout the organization.

Within an organization there needs to be an openness to change and innovation at all levels of the educational institution, not just with cutting edge technology, research, or forward-thinking professors in the classroom. This requires a vision that is shared and focused on continued steps to implement transformational change across the college or university. Not in an overwhelming way, but rather in a manner that encourages buy-in, confirms commitment, supports inclusion, and generates a sense of continued hope and excitement throughout the institution from both internal and external stakeholders.

The ability to innovate in higher education is a continual process. It is an imperative part of successfully educating students in today's hyper-competitive and ever-changing environment. This has been and will continue to be a strategic advantage and source of competitiveness for higher education.

An innovative mindset, combined with a high-performance culture that supports experimentation and new ideas, is essential for today's higher education leadership team. Many institutions are leaning more on faculty, staff, and students to define a shared vision toward needed change, while also encouraging diversity of thought in efforts to advance the initiatives of the institution.[14]

Colleges committed to innovation tend to be those committed to knowledge creation. Knowledge is an additional source of competitive advantage that should not be underestimated or weakened in this current environment. Knowledge within an educational institution is a resource provided by the immense amounts of human intellectual capital that exists throughout the different areas of academia.

As higher education continues to develop and change to adjust to the current needs of their communities, they must also manage their infrastructure in terms of how information flows and is managed throughout the organization. Infrastructure is the foundation of knowledge management and is a major organizational asset, influencing organizational behavior, culture, and overall learning.[15]

Effective communication is central to the organization. As institutional leaders think differently about the organization, there is need to create open communication. Communication that actively engages all members of the community to contribute from their own perspective and level of expertise. Including all members in the change process strengthens the leadership, culture, policies, processes, and structure of the overall institution.[16]

Successful leaders also have a strong future orientation and commitment to improvement and innovation.[17] For a future focused mindset to be successful, many leaders approach a problem through a process of "playing the movie backward" to put in place a vision that starts with the end in mind.[18]

This Understanding by Design framework can be used to construct institutional goals, complete assessments and data collection measures, and put in place activities needed to achieve intended institutional outcomes.[19] Throughout this process there is a level of transparency, so everyone knows what is expected and what is being sought.

Stakeholders are involved in the process with clearly communicated steps so that any issues or problems are dealt with along the way. Using a backward design approach allows leaders to visualize the outcome of the goals being set and then work in coordination with others in the institution to achieve its vision.

ORGANIZATIONAL AGILITY AND ADAPTATION

Just as faculty adjust and change as the teaching profession evolves, so too does the educational institution continually adapt to the contemporary social and economic needs of the community and the students in which it serves. In the present day as we emerge from the pandemic, there is an opportunity for higher education to advance.[20]

As institutional change efforts are underway, colleges must also work through the day-to-day institutional processes, such as accreditation and vetting of educational programs to ensure quality standards for the institution.

Quality aligns to high academic expectations and advocates rigor and scholastic standards for an education that is intellectually and personally challenging and which is defined by the vision, mission, and values of the institution as well as the standards of the faculty and programs offered.

There is a renewed focus on building a sense of community and student belonging across the campus whether classes and activities are in-person or virtual. This includes reinforcing institutional support and constructing levels of additional communication in such areas as program advising, career guidance, financial aid, social/emotional services, writing, speaking, and technology centers, as well as student-centered events and other places like dining and campus housing. This interwoven support is now more flexible in nature and more ubiquitous across the campus, whether in-person or online, thereby allowing institutions to serve and engage with students more frequently and consistently.

A strategic plan, one that encompasses the entire community and serves as a road map to guide day-to-day activities based on longer-term decisions and goals of the institution, is necessary to continually move the vision forward, advance the mission, ensure that values are upheld, and see that resultant goals and objectives are being implemented while also innovating and adhering to operational processes and accreditation standards.

For the twenty-first-century university, the organizational structure makes sense in terms of who-reports-to-whom and employees in general have a wide sense of autonomy and entrepreneurial acumen. They are encouraged to try new ideas and create improved opportunities for the students they serve.

Faculty and staff are supported even when they fail because novel innovations seldom come easily. Although there are members of the campus community who may feel left out from discussions and are seeking more voice in these efforts and support within the campus community.[21] They too need to be heard.

The best institutions of higher education have high levels of employee and student engagement and satisfaction. They recognize that there is a need to continually grow and innovate and to advance their practices around equity, diversity, and inclusion.

As faculty implement aspects of the institution's strategic plan and quality enhancement plans to improve student success into their coursework, they align to the mission and values of the institution while also supporting the goals of their discipline specific content and pedagogy.

By focusing on organizational agility, the campus community can come together, despite and in support of their different experiences and backgrounds, and the institution can move forward toward evidence-based change and the ability to work through issues comprehensively and equitably.[22]

COMMUNITY LEADERSHIP

Many educational leaders have been reluctant to speak out about issues important to their institution due to fear of offending constituents in their communities and state officials who are relied upon for institutional funding.[23]

Whether it is in defense of diversity, equity, or inclusion efforts, LGBTQ+ concerns, food or housing insecurity, or childcare and abortion, some college presidents are hesitant to show any signs of disagreement or uncertainty regarding their institution's stance.[24] This conflicts with the goal of higher education to provide a platform for scholarship, discussion, and social change.

Not being willing—or able—to discuss issues influencing and of concern in society limits the credibility of the educational institution in its growth toward change and renewal. It can also reflect negatively on providing opportunities for students to experiment, test new ideas, and dig deeper into topics that may be viewed as controversial. This type of open dialog is important and necessary to prepare students for life beyond the university and one where they are actively involved in their own new knowledge creation.[25]

A college president is often viewed as someone who has the capacity to bring everyone together. Whether it is students and faculty, alumni, donors, the board of trustees, state government officials, or community members, the university president soothes things over and makes everyone feel hopeful about where the institution is headed. Presidents hold a unique as well as vulnerable position within their respective institutions.[26]

Therefore, jumping into the fray of a Twitter frenzy is not something most presidents or educational leaders would relish. There is presently a need not to offend nor alienate the "friends" of the college who you need the most. This is accentuated by continuing financial issues brought on by the pandemic, enrollment declines, lack of state and national funding, and for some institutions, significant needed investments in infrastructure.

As of 2022, the top three stakeholders' college presidents reported worrying most about in terms of their criticism or critique were:

- politicians, especially elected officials in their state or local area;
- alumni, as they prefer the way the college was and may be the most resistant to change efforts; and
- faculty because of the passion of their responses.[27]

At the end of the day, shying away from a college's values or vision can have dire consequences. The risks are undermining the institution and its standing in the community as well as potentially having others see you as ineffectual.

Although no leader enjoys the controversy and possible repercussions of rebuttal or even termination, the unique nature of the position as a higher education leader requires the need to speak up about what is right and just in society. Moreover, the educational institution can serve as the conduit through which community members and students engage in civil dialog about issues and what it means to live in a democratic society.

As members of the educational influential, colleges and universities continually advance learning and knowledge to champion distinct identities, promote human rights, and ensure equal access around intellectual discussions across campus. It means showing up for difficult discussions using evidenced-based practices, defending facts, and holding stakeholders accountable.

LEADERSHIP FOR TOMORROW

Educational institutions are reimaging their campuses as they apply lessons learned from the pandemic. Opportunities exist for teaching and learning in different modalities and student choice is expanding with more adjustable options.[28]

As current times encourage new ideas and innovations, educational leadership must consider the organization's structure and framework to develop a unified strategy, one that incorporates an integrated understanding of the institution's mission and its strategic goals and objectives. To do this, there must be mutual understanding and cooperation internally, as well as with governing bodies, such as boards and state and federal interests, that promote learning and support the educational institution fully. Each must be considered as leaders work to promote the organizational changes necessary and move the institution forward.

MOVING FORWARD

Leadership is a conversation between key stakeholders that include college faculty and staff, students, and the long-term interests of the community. As we emerge from the pandemic, it is imperative that educational leadership embrace change and welcome the opportunities and challenges that lie ahead. Continual adjustments amid discussions with all stakeholders will ensure a viable, effective, and well-run organization that can handle the current environment and pivot seamlessly toward tomorrow.

Within this chapter, leadership qualities and the challenges that educational leaders currently face in higher education were explored. Following the pandemic, many university and college leaders are promoting transformative opportunities for change across their campuses even though they face multiple institutional pressures at the same time.

While the pandemic *was* difficult, it challenged society's thinking about education and is now providing educational leadership with an opportunity to rethink the system of higher education and their institution's place within it.[29]

NOTES

1. Chris Costa, "Six New England Colleges Close in 3 Years Leaving Students from Maine with Big Decisions," News Center Maine, April 26, 2019, https://www.newscentermaine.com/article/news/6-new-england-colleges-close-in-3-years-leaving-students-from-maine-stuck/97-c715d9f8-e11f-44c8-84c3-726bd8b42fd1.

2. Natalie Schwartz, "Are More College Closures Ahead?" Higher Ed Dive, April 1, 2021, https://www.highereddive.com/news/are-more-college-closures-ahead/597746/.

3. Ray Schroeder, "Imagine We Are Starting a University Now," Inside HigherEd, September 21, 2022, https://www.insidehighered.com/digital-learning/blogs/online-trending-now/imagine-we-are-starting-university-now.

4. "College and University Presidents Respond to COVID-19: 2021 Spring Term Survey," TIAA Institute, March 1, 2021, https://www.tiaa.org/public/institute/publication/2021/college-and-university-presidents-respond-covid-19-2021-spring-term-survey.

5. Gayle Greene, "The Liberal Arts Are Not Disposable," Nation of Change, May 24, 2021, https://www.nationofchange.org/2021/05/24/the-liberal-arts-are-not-disposable/.

6. Michael Connolly, Chris James, and Michael Fertig, "The Difference between Educational Management and Educational Leadership and the Importance of Educational Responsibility," *Educational Management Administration & Leadership* 47, no. 4 (2017): 504–19.

7. W. Warner Burke, *Organization Change: Theory and Practice* (Teachers College, Columbia University Press, 2017).

8. Alasdair Blair and Sarah Jones, "University Leaders Need to Demonstrate an Adaptive Mindset," *The Times Higher Education,* September 8, 2021, https://www.timeshighereducation.com/campus/university-leaders-need-demonstrate-adaptive-mindset.

9. Gregory A. Aarons, "Transformational and Transactional Leadership: Association with Attitudes toward Evidence-Based Practice," *Psychiatry Services* 57, no. 8 (2006): 1162–69.

10. Grayson Bodenheimer and Stef M. Shuster, "Emotional Labor. Teaching and Burnout: Investigating Complex Relationships," *Educational Research* 62, no. 1 (2019): 63–76.

11. Kevin R. McClure and Alisa Hicklin Fryar, "The Great Faculty Disengagement," *The Chronicle of Higher Education,* January 19, 2022, https://www.chronicle.com/article/the-great-faculty-disengagement.

12. Michelle B. Riba, Preeti N. Malani, Robert D. Ernst, and Sagar V. Parikh, "Mental Health on College Campuses: Supporting Faculty and Staff," *Psychiatric Times*, March 18, 2022, https://www.psychiatrictimes.com/view/mental-health-on-college-campuses-supporting-faculty-and-staff.

13. Matt Zalaznick, "COVID Layoffs, Furloughs Begin Hitting Colleges Hard," University Business, July 21, 2020, https://universitybusiness.com/covid-layoffs-furloughs-begin-hitting-colleges-hard/.

14. Theodore M. Hesburgh, "The Presidency: A Personalist Manifesto," 59th Annual Meeting of the American Council on Education, New Orleans, LA, October 7, 1976, https://archives.nd.edu/Hesburgh/CPHS142-09-07.pdf.

15. Peter Weill, Mani Subramani, and Marianne Broadbent, "Building IT Infrastructure for Strategic Agility," October 15, 2002, https://sloanreview.mit.edu/article/building-it-infrastructure-for-strategic-agility/.

16. Weill et al., "Building IT Infrastructure."

17. "Baldrige Criteria for Performance Excellence Categories and Items," NIST Baldrige Performance Excellence Program, 2023, https://www.nist.gov/baldrige/baldrige-criteria-commentary.

18. Helen Green, "The Ideas That Inspire Us," *Harvard Business Review*, November/December 2022, https://hbr.org/2022/11/the-ideas-that-inspire-us.

19. Grant P. Wiggins and Jay McTighe, *Understanding by Design* (Alexandra, VA: Association for Supervision and Curriculum Development, 2005).

20. Glenn Llopis, "Leading in a Time of Change: Higher Education in Transition," *Forbes*, November 23, 2022, https://www.forbes.com/sites/glennllopis/2022/11/23/leading-in-a-time-of-change-higher-education-in-transition/?sh=191893f71459.

21. Jeffrey Selingo, "Colleges Are Deeply Unequal Workplaces," *The Atlantic*, August 1, 2020, https://www.theatlantic.com/ideas/archive/2020/08/colleges-are-deeply-unequal-workplaces/614791/.

22. "Strengthening Trust in Focus," Aspen Global Leadership Network, 2023, https://www.aspeninstitute.org/programs/aspen-global-leadership-network/.

23. Eric Kelderman, "The Silent Treatment: Why College Presidents Don't Speak Out," *The Chronicle of Higher Education*, July 26, 2022, https://www.chronicle.com/article/the-silent-treatment.

24. Kelderman, "The Silent Treatment."

25. "What You Need to Know about Higher Education," UNESCO, January 16, 2023, https://www.unesco.org/en/higher-education/need-know#:~:text=Higher%20education%20is%20a%20rich,meet%20ever%20changing%20labour%20markets.

26. Kelderman, "The Silent Treatment."

27. Kelderman, "The Silent Treatment."

28. Jon Marcus, "A Handful of Colleges Are Finally Providing Training in a Way Consumers Want It: Fast," The Hechinger Report, December 14, 2021, https://hechingerreport.org/a-handful-of-colleges-are-finally-providing-training-in-a-way-consumers-want-it-fast/.

29. Marco Castiglioni and Nicolò Gaj, "Fostering the Reconstruction of Meaning among the General Population during the COVID-19 Pandemic," *Frontiers in Psychology* 11 (2020).

Chapter Ten

Reasons for Urgency

> *I believe that education is the fundamental method of social progress and reform.*
>
> —John Dewey, *The School Journal*

A sense of urgency is needed as we move forward in higher education. As educators strive to teach and motivate students about the world and their place in it, the ability for each student to see hope and opportunity is imperative.[1] As colleges and universities have been shaped throughout history based on events and changing world views, the lessons learned during the COVID-19 global health crisis have provided another occasion to observe significant advancements in educative practice.

The rate of change within higher education as well as other industries has been unrelenting. Prior to the pandemic in March 2020, the pace was fast, and during the pandemic there remained an atmosphere of change, albeit with different types of challenges.

In the present day, there is an engaged willingness to approach complex problems impacting the university and think forward to imagined improvements and opportunities of the future.[2] On today's college campuses, clear and concerted efforts are being made to establish deeper connections to the curriculum, foster diversity of thought, and engage students at higher levels to meet current universal challenges.

Educational leaders, faculty, and others who have dedicated their careers to higher education continue to work with students to instill knowledge, encourage innovation, and help them flourish in an unpredictable world where there is constant change and fluidity.

COMMITMENT TO HOPE

Lifelong students of today—*all of us*—must be open and accepting of change and committed to optimism and hope. Complacency is not an option in this new post-pandemic world and an imaginative and curious approach to problem solving and recognizing opportunities is needed as we move forward.

Today we are all tasked to be adaptable and flexible, as well as open to innovation and creativity using an entrepreneurial mindset. We face unprecedented transformations, and successfully navigating the pace of change and current uncertainty takes a unique set of emotional, social, and cognitive skills.[3]

Developing these skills can be accomplished through a liberal arts perspective emphasizing broad based knowledge along with the development of "soft" skills such as critical thinking, teamwork, problem solving, and communication, and through utilization of various teaching strategies discussed throughout this book.

The development of new ideas with a focus on making and creating are essential to transforming future opportunities for students, whether through socially responsible businesses, new-age technologies, or valuable community service. Through higher education, students are transformed in a manner that allows them to solve for problems and recognize opportunities.

The role of education is to open up the world for students to see these possibilities. To unleash their "can-do" attitude and "want-to" motivation that enables them to accomplish whatever it is they set their minds to. Within the college environment, students are challenged and engaged to think more deeply about issues and current events. Students develop more as citizens within the campus community whatever their age or occupation, and everyone at the college has a responsibility to help shape who they are becoming.

While skill advancement and learned knowledge are important, it is also critical to instill in each graduate a willingness to make the world a better place so that they can use their expertise and intellect to be of service and make a difference. Herein lies the true reward of education, not just for the individual but for society.

As a civilization, our goal is to ensure an improved future for all humanity. To do this, we need to be optimistic and far-reaching in our goal setting. We need to approach the future and our planning efforts collectively. And we must commit to hope and work together rather than apart. This requires discipline and patience to create a better future. We accomplish this through recognizing that we are all part of the change effort as we create experiences that teach students the importance of hard work, courage, and the tenacity to see things through. While new ideas will burst forth, they are accompanied by well-thought-out plans that include specific objectives to get things done.

In education as in life, it is helpful to remember that we are preparing students for jobs and life experiences that are unfolding in our current times and that are unknown at present. Thus, the real task is to instill in students the desire to be bold and to try and see things differently using critical and creative thinking along with an inquiry-minded approach. By doing this, the entire educational system will continually grow and evolve to accomplish new inventions and innovations that before had been thought impossible.

In effecting change and opening students up to the possibilities of new ideas and creative options, there must be institutional support to help guide their critical examination through campus-wide collaboration and connections. When an institution has as its mission to prepare students to actively tackle challenges, ask and pursue important questions, and translate research into action, they must also consider an interdisciplinary approach that connects diverse voices and uses a constructivist and inquiry-oriented mindset as discussed throughout this text.

This constructive and inquiry-oriented approach supports flexibility and adaptability in advancing knowledge that leads to the potential for creative solutions. The goal is to create a community doing the difficult work of learning from past experiences while also focused on the future with the positive actions and critical awareness to not just remain relevant, but to truly excel in advancing higher education into the "new normal."

EDUCATION MATTERS

As we move forward post-pandemic, higher education continues to benefit nations, communities, and the students they serve. A college degree remains the most dependable and reliable route to economic security. In the challenging times created by the pandemic and simultaneous world events, employees with higher levels of education still tend to earn more and have lower rates of unemployment when compared with employees with less education.[4]

In the next decade, it is projected that of the 35 million job openings in the United States, 40 percent will be to those with college degrees, followed by 30 percent to those with some postsecondary training.[5] Whether through the traditional four-year or two-year college degree or other more short-term credentialed opportunities for learning, it is time to redefine success and what that means to students in this new world they will inherit.

The benefits afforded by education are numerous as it can

- boost confidence and hope,
- build empathy and tolerance,
- promote independent thought,
- inspire problem solving,
- build communication,
- open doors,
- reduce poverty,
- increase political and community involvement, and
- cultivate respect.[6]

The "new normal" is predicated on a growth mindset, one that is open to transformation, even when we are not sure what that will look like. The ability to accept risk and uncertainty to access prosperity through challenge, and seek opportunities based on planning and sound judgment of possibilities.

While the pandemic may have redefined the college experience and what it means to be a college student, going forward the role of innovation and creativity will determine our level of contribution and ability to problem solve.

PLANNING FOR THE FUTURE

The COVID-19 pandemic changed us, but we also realize that disruptions are constant and through effective planning, colleges and universities can prepare for the unknown by being proactive rather than reactive.

In early 2020, institutions of higher education responded quickly using the best options available to move through the phases of the pandemic. By incorporating contingency planning into day-to-day operations, college leadership completed the advanced preparation necessary so that the most logical and careful decision making could occur.

Our new reality is focused on ensuring rigorous, equitable, and thoughtful learning opportunities in various instructional modes that we can pivot to when needed.[7] Having a plan and built-in systems to help the organization move seamlessly between remote and in-person instruction, as well as devoting resources so that students feel a part of the institution, the educative process, and the academic environment is key.

Setting up these solutions now and building new models and frameworks will help institutions share best practices and collaborate internally up and down the organizational structure, as well as with other educational institutions nationally and internationally. While an organic organizational structure for higher education is helpful, a culture of experimentation, acceptance of mistakes, and encouragement of new ideas is paramount.

The best organizations provide the time, space, and autonomy for their employees *to think* so that they can be mentally centered and offer creative solutions to problems. While there are always priorities, initiatives, and requirements to be completed, the educational institutions that embrace a culture of innovation provide employees with the time needed to process through complex issues that are organizationally or student focused.

As educational leaders consider this moment post-pandemic, they are taking bold steps to reinvent the future of higher education. In so doing, they are critically analyzing their vision of the campus community and how they see new opportunities as we move toward an improved higher education experience.

In this realignment process, a variety of stakeholder groups are brought together to create an inclusive environment to effectuate the relevant change that is needed for our times. To engage these collective voices and being willing to listen and act, we create stronger collaborative relationships across the college campus, thereby building a sustained and engaged community of higher education that is optimistic, hopeful, and emboldened.

While higher education is not broken, it could do with a few repairs. The pandemic has shined a light on higher education. While the pandemic has been life-changing and invoked obstacles not previously experienced during this lifetime, it has also exposed issues not formerly known. In this way, the crisis has also been an opportunity for change and renewal.

The biggest question for change leaders in higher education is how to move forward with transformative efforts that make sense for the institution and for these times. It is an exciting time to be in higher education post-pandemic. Fasten your seatbelt and enjoy the ride for the betterment of educational leadership, faculty and staff, students, and the communities they serve.

MOVING FORWARD

It is our hope that this text has furthered your thoughts about higher education during this evolutionary period as well as instilled a sense of optimism and confidence to engage in the work needed to strengthen and extend the future of higher education. At present, there is tremendous potential to address and create pathways to professional and personal success for a wide variety and diversity of students.

To actively engage students' wonder for the world around them is one of the greatest gifts higher education can provide. Today's students come into higher education with varying dreams and desires, as well as levels of intellect and drive. Students want to learn and apply their knowledge to the best of their abilities to this current and complex world.

How big and multidimensional issues are approached over the next decade will define the United States as a country and as a generation.[8] How these problems are solved will determine our future. Those who do not seek out knowledge or who object regarding the long-term existence of higher education are advancing a nation toward oppression and absolutism. The stakes are high, and the bar must be reached.

Right now, we have an opportunity to make a substantial impact on current and future generations. Students in higher education must be able to think critically about problems. They need to work collaboratively toward bold solutions and possibilities with an innovative and creative mindset. They must ask questions and use inquiry to make a difference in people lives by eliciting positive global change for the world in which we all live. The continuation of our civil and democratic society depends on it.

NOTES

1. Tom Hanks, "I Owe It All to Community College," January 14, 2015, *The New York Times*, https://www.nytimes.com/2015/01/14/opinion/tom-hanks-on-his-two-years-at-chabot-college.html.

2. Ann M. Pendleton-Jullian and John Seely Brown, *Design Unbound: Designing for Emergence in a White Water World* (Cambridge, MA: The MIT Press, 2018).

3. Gabriella Rosen Kellerman and Martin E. P. Seligman, "There's a Mental Health Crisis at Work Because Life Is Changing Too Fast," *Time*, January 24, 2023, https://time.com/6249306/work-mental-health-crisis-life-changes/.

4. Elka Torpey, "Education Pays, 2020," U.S. Bureau of Labor Statistics *Career Outlook*, June 2021, https://www.bls.gov/careeroutlook/2021/data-on-display/education-pays.htm.

5. Karin Fischer, "The Shrinking of Higher Ed," *The Chronicle of Higher Education*, August 12, 2022, https://www-chronicle-com.umw.idm.oclc.org/article/the-shrinking-of-higher-ed.

6. "Education for Peace: Top 10 Ways Education Promotes Peace," Asia Institute Education Promotes Peace Central, December 23, 2017, https://centralasiainstitute.org/top-10-ways-education-promotes-peace/.

7. Javeria Salman, "How to Plan for a Future of Education Where Disruption is the Norm," The Hechinger Report, January 5, 2022, https://hechingerreport.org/how-to-plan-for-a-future-of-education-where.

8. Helen L. Walls, "Wicked Problems and a 'Wicked' Solution," *Global Health* 14, no. 34 (2018).

Bibliography

117th U.S. Congress. *S.5108 – Housing for Homeless Students Act of 2022*. Washington, DC: U.S. Congress.

"2021 Social and Emotional Learning Report." McGraw Hill. 2021. http://mheducation.com/sel-survey.

Aarons, Gregory A. "Transformational and Transactional Leadership: Association with Attitudes toward Evidence-Based Practice." *Psychiatry Services* 57, no. 8 (2006): 1162–69.

Abad, Mark, and McDowell, Erin. "The Oldest College in Every US State." *Insider*. 2018. https://www.businessinsider.com/oldest-college-every-state-2018-10.

"About Learning Evaluations." American Council on Education (ACE). 2022. https://www.acenet.edu/Programs-Services/Pages/Credit-Transcripts/About-Learning-Evaluation.aspx.

Abrams, Gina Baral, and Joshua Wachtel. "During the COVID-19 Crisis, Restorative Practices Can Help." International Institute for Restorative Practices Graduate School. March 24, 2020. https://www.iirp.edu/news/during-the-covid-19-crisis-restorative-practices-can-help.

Alexander, Brian. "What Might ChatGPT Mean for Higher Education?" YouTube. https://youtu.be/Bz7aW6vStBw.

Alonso, Johanna. "How Higher Ed Can Help Remedy K–12 Learning Loss." Inside Higher Ed. October 26, 2022. https://www.insidehighered.com/news/2022/10/26/colleges-can-help-k-12-schools-combat-pandemic-learning-loss.

Álvarez, Brenda. "Why Social Justice in School Matters." *NeaToday*. January 22, 2019. https://www.nea.org/advocating-for-change/new-from-nea/why-social-justice-school-matters.

Ambrose, Susan A., Michael W. Bridges, Marsha C. Lovett, Michele DiPietro, and Marie K. Norman. *How Learning Works: 7 Research-Based Principles for Smart Teaching*. San Francisco, CA: Josey-Bass, 2010.

"American Association of Community Colleges Puts Spotlight on CSM's Mission, COVID-19 Response." College of Southern Maryland. December 3, 2020. https://

www.csmd.edu/news/2020/12/american-association-of-community-colleges-puts-spotlight-on-csms-mission,-covid-19-response.html.

Anderson, Janna, Lee Raine, and Emily A. Vogels. "Experts Say the 'New Normal' in 2025 Will Be Far More Tech-Driven, Presenting More Big Challenges." Pew Research Center. February 18, 2021. https://www.pewresearch.org/internet/2021/02/18/experts-say-the-new-normal-in-2025-will-be-far-more-tech-driven-presenting-more-big-challenges/.

Angelo, Thomas P., and K. Patricia Cross. *Classroom Assessment Techniques: A Handbook for College Teachers.* San Francisco: Jossey-Bass, 1993.

Antony, Jiju. "A SWOT Analysis on Six Sigma: Some Perspectives from Leading Academic and Practitioners." *International Journal of Productivity and Performance Management* 61, no. 6 (2012).

Ardeni, Viola, Sara Dallavalle, and Karolina Serafin. "Building Student Communities in Spite of the COVID-19 Pandemic." *Journal of Teaching and Learning with Technology Special Issue* 10 (2021): 88–102.

Aristovnik, Alexsander, Damijana Kerzic, Dejan Ravselj, Nina Tomazevic, and Lan Umek. "Impacts of the COVID-19 Pandemic on Life of Higher Education Students: A Global Perspective." *Sustainability 12*, no. 20 (2020).

Arum, Richard, and Mitchell L. Stevens. "Building Tomorrow's Workforce Today: Twin Proposals for the Future of Learning, Opportunity, and Work." Hamilton Project. 2020. https://www.hamiltonproject.org/assets/files/PP_ArumStevens_LO_FINAL.pdf.

"Auxiliary Aids and Services for Postsecondary Students with Disabilities." U.S. Department of Education. https://www2.ed.gov/about/offices/list/ocr/docs/auxaids.html.

"Bachelors to Graduate Degree Accelerated Programs." University of Mary Washington Partner Programs. January 21, 2023. https://cas.umw.edu/beyond/partnership-programs/.

Bada, S. O., and Steve Olusegun. "Constructivism Learning Theory: A Paradigm for Teaching and Learning." *Journal of Research & Method in Education 5*, no. 6 (2015): 66–70.

Baer, Linda L., Ann Hill Duin, and Judith A. Ramaley. "Smart Change." *Planning for Higher Education* 36, no. 2 (2008): 5–16.

Bailey, Rebecca, Emily A. Meland, Gretchen Brion-Meisels, and Stephanie M. Jones. "Getting Developmental Science Back into Schools: Can What We Know about Self-Regulation Help Change How We Think about 'No Excuses'?" *Frontiers Psychology* 10 (2019).

"Baldrige Criteria for Performance Excellence Categories and Items." NIST Baldrige Performance Excellence Program. 2023. https://www.nist.gov/baldrige/baldrige-criteria-commentary.

Barkley, Elizabeth F., and Claire Howell Major. *Engaged Teaching: A Handbook for College Faculty.* The K. Patricia Cross Academy, 2022.

Barrett-Fox, Rebecca. "Please Do a Bad Job of Putting Your Courses Online." March 2020. https://anygoodthing.com/2020/03/12/please-do-a-bad-job-of-putting-your-courses-online/.

Barshay, Jill. "College Students Predicted to Fall by More than 15% after the Year 2025," Hechinger Report. September 10, 2018. https://hechingerreport.org/college-students-predicted-to-fall-by-more-than-15-after-the-year-2025/.

Barshay, Jill. "COVID-19 Has Been Bad for College Enrollment – But Awful for Community College Students." The Hechinger Report. October 26, 2020. https://hechingerreport.org/high-school-graduates-shun-college-in-the-covid-fall-of-2020/.

Barshay, Jill. "Why So Few Students Transfer from Community Colleges to Four-Year Universities." The Hechinger Report. June 2020. https://hechingerreport.org/why-so-few-students-transfer-from-commun.

Bateman, Walter L. *Open to Question: The Art of Teaching and Learning by Inquiry*. San Francisco, Jossey-Bass, 1990.

Bauld, Andrew. "What Is Inquiry-Based Learning?" Rethink Together. February 14, 2022. https://xqsuperschool.org/rethinktogether/what-is-inquiry-based-learning-ibl/.

Baum, Sandy, Charles Kurose, and Jennifer Ma. "How College Shapes Lives: Understanding the Issues." College Board. October 2013. https://research.collegeboard.org/media/pdf/education-pays-how-college-shapes-lives-report.pdf.

Beatty, Brian J. *Hybrid-Flexible Course Design*. Self-Published EdTech Books, 2019.

Beauchamp, Justin, Emily Schwartz, and Elizabeth Davidson Pisacreta. "Seven Practices for Building Community and Student Belonging Virtually." *The Chronicle of Higher Education*. May 13, 2021. https://www.chronicle.com/professional-development/report/seven-practices-for-building-community-and-student-belonging-virtually.

Beheshti, Naz. "We Can No Longer Ignore Burnout Syndrome Related to Chronic Stress, Says World Health Organization." *Forbes*. June 10, 2019. https://www.forbes.com/sites/nazbeheshti/2019/06/10/we-can-no-longer-ignore-burnout-syndrome-related-to-chronic-stress-says-world-health-organization/?sh=76599cd56a37.

Bergan, Sjur. "How Universities Can Promote 'Democratic Competences' among Students." Times Higher Education. March 24, 2022. https://www.timeshighereducation.com/campus/how-universities-can-promote-democratic-competences-among-students.

Bichsel, Jacqueline, Melissa Fuesting, Jennifer Schneider, and Diana Tubbs. "The CUPA-HR 2022 Higher Education Employee Retention Survey: Initial Results." College and University Professional Association for Human Resources. July 2022. https://www.cupahr.org/surveys/research-briefs/higher-ed-employee-retention-survey-findings-july-2022/.

Blair, Alasdair, and Sarah Jones. "University Leaders Need to Demonstrate an Adaptive Mindset." *The Times Higher Education*. September 8, 2021. https://www.timeshighereducation.com/campus/university-leaders-need-demonstrate-adaptive-mindset.

Bodenheimer, Grayson, and Stef M. Shuster. "Emotional Labor. Teaching and Burnout: Investigating Complex Relationships." *Educational Research* 62, no. 1 (2019): 63–76.

Bonem, Emily M., Heather Fedesco, and Angelika N. Zissimopoulos. "What You Do Is Less Important Than How you Do It: The Effects of Learning Environments on Student Outcomes." *Learning Environments Research 23* (2020): 27–44.

Bringle, Robert G., and Julie A. Hatcher. "Institutionalization of Service Learning in Higher Education." *The Journal of Higher Education* 71, no. 3 (2000).

Brooks, Jacqueline Grennon, and Martin G. Brooks. *In Search of Understanding: The Case for Constructivist Classrooms.* Alexandria, VA: American Society for Curriculum Development, 1999.

Bruner, John. *Acts of Meaning.* Cambridge, MA: Harvard University Press, 1990.

Buckwalter-Arias, James. "Liberal Education after the Pandemic." American Association of University Professors. Fall 2020. https://www.aaup.org/article/liberal-education-after-pandemic#.Y8QjG-zMKRw.

"Building the Future of Education." OECD. 2023. https://www.oecd.org/education/future-of-education-brochure.pdf.

Burke, Warner W. *Organization Change: Theory and Practice.* Teachers College, Columbia University Press, 2017.

Cameron, Ryan M. Why High-Tech and Education Partnerships Work. LinkedIn. October 1, 2019. https://www.linkedin.com/pulse/why-high-tech-higher-education-partnerships-work-ryan-m-cameron.

Campbell, Leah. "Impact of COVID-19 on Children's Social Skills." *Forbes.* October 31, 2021). https://www.forbes.com/sites/leahcampbell/2021/10/31/impact-of-covid-19-on-childrens-social-skills.

"CARES Act." U.S. Department of Education Office of Postsecondary Education. https://www2.ed.gov/about/offices/list/ope/caresact.html.

Carlton, Genevieve. "Higher Education and Pandemics." Best Colleges. May 11, 2022. https://www.bestcolleges.com/blog/higher-education-and-pandemics/.

Carnevale, Anthony P., Ban Cheah, and Emma Wenzinger. "The College Payoff: More Education Doesn't Always Mean More Earnings." Georgetown University Center on Education and the Workforce. 2021. https://cewgeorgetown.wpenginepowered.com/wp-content/uploads/cew-college_payoff_2021-fr.pdf.

Carnevale, Anthony P., Tamara Jayasundera, and Artem Gulish. "America's Divided Recovery: College Haves and Have-Nots." Georgetown University Center on Education and the Workforce. 2016. https://cewgeorgetown.wpenginepowered.com/wp-content/uploads/Americas-Divided-Recovery-web.pdf.

Carnevale, Anthony P., and Stephen J. Rose. "The Economy Goes to College: The Hidden Promise of Higher Education in the Post-Industrial Service Economy," Georgetown University Center on Education and The Workforce. 2015. https://cewgeorgetown.wpenginepowered.com/wp-content/uploads/EconomyGoesToCollege.pdf.

Castiglioni, Marco, and Nicolò Gaj. "Fostering the Reconstruction of Meaning Among the General Population during the COVID-19 Pandemic." *Frontiers in Psychology* 11 (2020).

Chen, Stefanos. "A New Lifeline for the Unseen: Homeless College Students." *New York Times.* December 2022. https://www.nytimes.com/2022/12/18/realestate/college-housing-homeless-students.html.

"CHLOE 7: Tracking Online Learning from Mainstream Acceptance to Universal Adoption: The Changing Landscape of Online Education." *Encoura*. 2022. https://encoura.org/project/chloe-7/.

Choo, Chun Wei. *The Management of Learning: Organizations as Knowledge-Creating Enterprises*. Oxford Academic, 2005.

Coffman, Teresa. *Inquiry-Based Learning: Designing Instruction to Promote Higher Level Thinking*. Lanham, MD: Rowman & Littlefield, 2017.

"College and University Presidents Respond to COVID-19: 2021 Spring Term Survey." March 1, 2021. https://www.tiaa.org/public/institute/publication/2021/college-and-university-presidents-respond-covid-19-2021-spring-term-survey.

"Mapping Upward: Stackable Credentials That Lead to Careers." U.S. Department of Education Office of Career Technical and Adult Education. December 2022. https://cte.ed.gov/initiatives/community-college-stackable-credentials.

Conklin, Sheri, and Amy Garrett Dikkers. "Instructor Social Presence and Connectedness in a Quick Shift from Face-To-Face to Online Instruction." *Online Learning* 25, no. 1 (2021).

Connolly, Michael, Chris James, and Michael Fertig. "The Difference between Educational Management and Educational Leadership and the Importance of Educational Responsibility," *Educational Management Administration & Leadership* 47, no. 4 (2017): 504–19.

Copley, Paul, and Edward Douthett. "Mega-Universities, COVID-19, and the Changing Landscapes of U.S. Colleges." *The CPA Journal*, October 2020.

Cortés, Julián D., Liliana Rivera, and Katerina Bohle Carbonelld. "Mission Statements in Universities: Readability and Performance." *European Research on Management and Business Economics* 28, no. 2 (2022).

Costa, Chris. "Six New England Colleges Close in 3 Years Leaving Students from Maine with Big Decisions." News Center Maine. April 26, 2019. https://www.newscentermaine.com/article/news/6-new-england-colleges-close-in-3-years-leaving-students-from-maine-stuck/97-c715d9f8-e11f-44c8-84c3-726bd8b42fd1.

Costello, Bob, Joshua Wachetel, and Ted Wachtel. *The Restorative Practices Handbook: for Teachers, Disciplinarians and Administrators*. Bethlehem, PA: International Institute for Restorative Practices, 2009.

"COVID-19 Data Review: Update on COVID-19–Related Mortality." Centers for Disease Control and Prevention. January 15, 2023. https://www.cdc.gov/coronavirus/2019-ncov/science/data-review/index.html.

"COVID-19 Mortality Overview," CDC National Center for Health Statistics 2022. https://www.cdc.gov/nchs/covid19/mortality-overview.htm.

Cox, Geoffrey M. *Theorizing the Resilience of American Higher Education: How Colleges and Universities Adapt to Changing Social and Economic Conditions*. London, UK: Routledge, 2020.

Cross, K. Patricia, Elizabeth F. Barkley, and Claire H. Major. *Collaborative Learning Techniques: A Handbook for College Faculty*. San Francisco, CA: Jossey-Bass, 2014.

Crown, Judith. "Confronting the Cliff: A Declining School-Age Population Leaves Small Colleges at a Crossroads." *Crain's Chicago Business*. August 26, 2022.

https://www.chicagobusiness.com/crains-forum-higher-education/colleges-universities-student-population-enrollment-cliff.

Cullinan, Dan, and Elizabeth Kopko. "Lessons from Two Experimental Studies of Multiple Measures Assessment." Center for the Analysis of Postsecondary Readiness. January 2022. https://postsecondaryreadiness.org/wp-content/uploads/2022/01/multiple-measures-assessment-reflections.pdf.

"Cultural Responsive Teaching: A Guide to Evidence-Based Practices for Teaching All Students Equitably." Education Northwest: Region X Equity Assistance Center. March 2016. https://educationnorthwest.org/sites/default/files/resources/culturally-responsive-teaching.pdf.

Curwin. Richard L., "Create a Partnership with Your Students When Designing Your Social Contract," *ASCD*. April 25, 2014. https://www.ascd.org/blogs/create-a-partnership-with-your-students-when-designing-your-social-contract.

Dabbagh, Nada, Rose M. Marra, and Jane L. Howland. *Meaningful Online Learning: Integrating Strategies, Activities, and Learning Technologies for Effective Designs.* London: Routledge, 2018.

Davidson, Neil, and Toni Worsham. *Enhancing Thinking through Cooperative Learning.* New York: Teachers College Press, 1992.

Dewey, John. *Experience and Education.* Toronto: Collier-MacMillan Canada Ltd., 1938.

Dewey, John. *How We Think: A Restatement of the Relation of Reflective Thinking to the Educative Process.* Lexington, MA: D.C. Heath and Company, 1933.

Diaz-Infante, Nadine, Michael Lazar, Samvitha Ram, and Austin Ray. "Demand for Online Education Is Growing. Are Providers Ready?" McKinsey & Company. https://www.mckinsey.com/industries/education/our-insights/demand-for-online-education-is-growing-are-providers-ready.

Diaz, Kim. "Paulo Freire (1921–1997)." Internet Encyclopedia of Philosophy. https://iep.utm.edu/freire/.

"Digest of Education Statistics." Table 311.15, "Number and Percentage of Students Enrolled in Degree-Granting Postsecondary Institutions, by Distance Education Participation, Location of Student, Level of Enrollment, and Control and Level of Institution: Fall 2017 and Fall 2018." National Center for Education Statistics Institute of Education Sciences, 2020. Washington, DC.

DLINQ Staff Contributors. *The Asynchronous Cookbook*. Self-Published Open Textbook Library, 2021.

Dolan, Simon L., Mario Raich, Anat Garti, and Avishai Landau, A. "The COVID-19 Crisis as an Opportunity for Introspection: A Multi-Level Reflection on Values, Needs, Trust and Leadership in the Future." *The European Business Review*. August 6, 2020. https://www.europeanbusinessreview.com/the-covid-19-crisis-as-an-opportunity-for-introspection/.

Dondi, Macro, Julia Klier, Frédéric Panier, and Jörg Schubert. "Defining the Skills Citizens Will Need in the Future World of Work." McKinsey & Company. June 21, 2021. https://www.mckinsey.com/industries/public-and-social-sector/our-insights/defining-the-skills-citizens-will-need-in-the-future-world-of-work?/

Donovan, M. Suzanne, John D. Bransford, and James W. Pellegrino. *How People Learn: Brain, Mind, Experience, and School*. Washington, DC: The National Academies Press, 2000.

Driscoll, Marcy P., and Kerry J. Burner. *Psychology of Learning for Instruction*. Hoboken, NJ: Pearson, 2022.

Drozdowski, Mark J. "Google, Microsoft Promote Tech Careers through Community Colleges." Best Colleges. May 6, 2022. https://www.bestcolleges.com/news/analysis/2021/11/15/google-microsoft-tech-careers-community-colleges/.

"Dual Enrollment Research: A Comprehensive Review." Southern Regional Education Board. June 2020. https://www.sreb.org/sites/main/files/file-attachments/dual_enrollment_2020.pdf.

Durlak, Joseph A., Roger P. Weissberg, Allison B. Dymnicki, and Rebecca D. Taylor. "The Impact of Enhancing Students' Social and Emotional Learning: A Meta-Analysis of School-Based Universal Interventions." *Child Development* 82, no 1. (2011): 405–32.

Dweck, Carol S. *Mindset: The New Psychology of Success*. New York: Ballantine Books, 2016.

Dyer, Becky, and T. Löytönen. "Engaging Dialogue: Co-Creating Communities of Collaborative Inquiry." *Research in Dance Education 13*, no. 1 (2011): 121–47.

Edmondson, Amy C. "Strategies for Learning from Failure." *Harvard Business Review*. April 2011. https://hbr.org/2011/04/strategies-for-learning-from-failure.

"Education for Peace: Top 10 Ways Education Promotes Peace." Asia Institute Education Promotes Peace Central. December 23, 2017. https://centralasiainstitute.org/top-10-ways-education-promotes-peace/.

"Education in a Pandemic: The Disparate Impacts of COVID-19 on America's Students." Department of Education Office for Civil Rights. June 9, 2021. https://www2.ed.gov/about/offices/list/ocr/docs/20210608-impacts-of-covid19.pdf.

Evans, Carla. "Instructing and Assessing 21st Century Skills: A Focus on Collaboration." Center for Assessment. November 13, 2021. https://www.nciea.org/blog/instructing-assessing-21st-century-skills-a-focus-on-collaboration/.

"Fact Sheet: The U.S. Department of Education Announces Partnerships across States, School Districts, and Colleges of Education to Meet Secretary Cardona's Call to Action to Address the Teacher Shortage." U.S. Department of Education. January 21, 2023. https://www.ed.gov/coronavirus/factsheets/teacher-shortage.

Ferlazzo, Larry. "Ways to Implement Restorative Practices in the Classroom." *Education Week*, January 9, 2020, https://www.edweek.org/teaching-learning/opinion-ways-to-implement-restorative-practices-in-the-classroom/2020/01.

Fischer, Christian, Zachary A. Pardos, Ryan Shaun Baker, Joseph Jay Williams, Padraic Smyth, Renzhe Yu, Stefan Slater, Rachel Baker, and Marc Warschauer. "Mining Big Data in Education: Affordances and Challenges." *Review of Research in Education* 44, no. 1 (2020): 130–60.

Fischer, Karin. "The Shrinking of Higher Ed." *The Chronicle of Higher Education*. August 12, 2022. https://www-chronicle-com.umw.idm.oclc.org/article/the-shrinking-of-higher-ed.

"Framework for 21st Century Learning." Battelle for Kids. 2019. https://static.battelleforkids.org/documents/p21/P21_Framework_Brief.pdf.

Francescucci, Anthony, and Mary Foster. "The VIRI (Virtual, Interactive, Real-Time, Instructor-Led) Classroom: The Impact of Blended Synchronous Online Courses on Student Performance, Engagement, and Satisfaction." *Canadian Journal of Higher Education* 43, no. 3 (2013): 78–91.

Freedman, Paul, and Paul LeBlanc. "Let's Make This the 'Year of Stackability.'" Inside Higher Ed. June 11, 2021. https://www.insidehighered.com/views/2021/06/11/credentials-must-be-stackable-if-were-educate-adult-learners-successfully-opinion.

Freire, Paulo. *Pedagogy of the Oppressed*. New York: Continuum, 1970.

Fuesting, Melissa, Sarah Nadel-Hawhthorn, Anthony Schmidt, and Jacqueline Bischsel. "Professionals in Higher Education Annual Report: Key Findings, Trends, and Comprehensive Tables for the 2020–21 Academic Year Overview." College and University Professional Association for Human Resources. 2021.

"Fundamentals of SEL." CASEL: Collaborative for Academic, Social, and Emotional Learning. 2022. https://casel.org/fundamentals-of-sel/.

"FY 2021 Data and Statistics. Apprenticeship. Employment and Training Administration." U.S. Department of Labor, 2021, https://www.dol.gov/agencies/eta/apprenticeship/about/statistics/2021.

Garrison, Randy D., and Norman D. Vaughan. *Blended Learning in Higher Education: Framework, Principles, and Guidelines*. San Francisco, CA: Wiley Jossey-Bass, 2012.

Garvin, David A. "Building a Learning Organization." *Harvard Business Review*. July-August 1993. https://hbr.org/1993/07/building-a-learning-organization.

Gates, Sabrina. "Benefits of Collaboration." National Education Association. October 18, 2018. https://www.nea.org/professional-excellence/student-engagement/tools-tips/benefits-collaboration.

Geary, Chris. "College Pays Off. But By How Much Depends on Race, Gender, and Type of Degree." *New America*. March 1, 2022. https://www.newamerica.org/education-policy/edcentral/college-pays-off/.

"Global Social Mobility Index 2020: Why Economies Benefit from Fixing Inequality." World Economic Forum. January 19, 2020. https://www.weforum.org/reports/global-social-mobility-index-2020-why-economies-benefit-from-fixing-inequality/.

Gobel, Reyna. "The Benefits of an Accelerated Bachelor's/Master's Degree." Investopedia. December 10, 2022. https://www.investopedia.com/articles/professionaleducation/11/accelerated-bachelors-masters-degree.asp.

Golembeski, Dean. "Amazon Invests in Community College Bachelor's Degree Programs." Best Colleges. January 24, 2022. https://www.bestcolleges.com/news/2022/01/24/amazon-washington-community-colleges-computer-science/.

Goodsell, Anne S., Michelle R. Maher, and Vincent Tinto. *Collaborative Learning: A Sourcebook for Higher Education*. University Park, PA: National Center on Postsecondary Teaching, Learning, and Assessment, 1992.

Goudeau, Sébastien, Camille Sanrey, Arnaud Stanczak, Antony Manstead, and Céline Darnon. "Why Lockdown and Distance Learning during the COVID-19 Pandemic Are Likely to Increase the Social Class Achievement Gap." *Nature Human Behaviour* 5 (2021): 1273–81.
Grajek, Susan, and D. Christopher Brooks. "How Technology Can Support Student Success during COVID-19." *Educause*. March 24, 2020. https://er.educause.edu/blogs/2020/3/how-technology-can-support-student-success-during-covid19.
Grant, Adam. "Burnout Isn't Just in Your Head. It's in Your Circumstances." *The New York Times,* March 19, 2020. https://www.nytimes.com/2020/03/19/smarter-living/coronavirus-emotional-support.html.
Grant, Adam, and Reb Rebele. "Beat Generosity Burnout." *Harvard Business Review*. January 23, 2017. https://hbr.org/2017/01/beat-generosity-burnout.
Green, Helen. "The Ideas That Inspire Us." *Harvard Business Review*. November /December 2022. https://hbr.org/2022/11/the-ideas-that-inspire-us.
Greene, Gayle. "The Liberal Arts Are Not Disposable." Nation of Change. May 24, 2021. https://www.nationofchange.org/2021/05/24/the-liberal-arts-are-not-disposable/.
Guilford, Joy P. "Creativity: Yesterday, Today and Tomorrow." *The Journal of Creative Behavior* 1, no. 1 (1967): 3–14.
Hanks, Tom. "I Owe It All to Community College." January 14, 2015. *The New York Times.* https://www.nytimes.com/2015/01/14/opinion/tom-hanks-on-his-two-years-at-chabot-college.html.
Harrison, Spencer, Elizabeth D. Rouse, Colin M. Fisher, and Teresa M. Amabile. "The Turn toward Creative Work." *Academy of Management Collections* 1, no. 1 (2022): 1–15.
Hattie, John. *Visible Learning: A Synthesis of Over 800 Meta-Analysis Relating to Achievement*. London: Routledge, 2009.
Hawes, Carrie, and Samara Reynolds. "Radical Retention: How Higher Education Can Rise to the Challenges of the Great Resignation and Beyond." National Association of Colleges and Employers., August 1, 2022. https://www.naceweb.org/career-development/best-practices/radical-retention-how-higher-education-can-rise-to-the-challenges-of-the-great-resignation-and-beyond/.
He, Wenliang, Daniel Gajski, George Farkas, and Mark Warschauer. "Implementing Flexible Hybrid Instruction in an Electrical Engineering Course: The Best of Three Worlds?" *Computers & Education* 81 (2015): 59–68.
Hehir, Elizabeth, Marc Zeller, Joanna Luckhurst, and Tara Chandler. "Developing Student Connectedness under Remote Learning Using Digital Resources: A Systematic Review." *Education and Information Technologies* 26 (2021): 6531–48.
Heng, Yu Tse, and Kira Schabram. "Your Burnout Is Unique. Your Recovery Will Be, Too." *Harvard Business Review*. April 12, 2021. https://hbr.org/2021/04/your-burnout-is-unique-your-recovery-will-be-too.
Herlambang, Mega B., Fokie Cnossen, and Niels A. Taatgen. "The Effects of Intrinsic Motivation on Mental Fatigue." *PLos One* 16, no. 1 (2021).

Herold, Benjamin. "How Tech-Driven Teaching Strategies Have Changed during the Pandemic." *Education Week*. April 14, 2022. https://www.edweek.org/technology/how-tech-driven-teaching-strategies-have-changed-during-the-pandemic/2022/04.

Hesburgh, Theodore M. "The Presidency: A Personalist Manifesto." 59th Annual Meeting of the American Council on Education. New Orleans, LA, October 7, 1976. https://archives.nd.edu/Hesburgh/CPHS142-09-07.pdf.

"High-Impact Practices." American Association of Colleges and Universities. January 1, 2023. https://www.aacu.org/trending-topics/high-impact.

Hirsch, Paddy. "How the Pandemic Changed the Rules of Personal Finance." National Public Radio. January 31, 2023. https://www.npr.org/sections/money/2023/01/31/1152162432/how-the-pandemic-changed-the-rules-of-personal-finance.

Hirsch, Sidney, and Lawrence C. Shulman. "Participatory Governance: A Model for Shared Decision Making." *Social Work in Health Care* 1, no. 4 (1976): 433–46.

Hirumi, Atsusi. *Grounded Designs for Online and Hybrid Learning: Design Fundamentals*. International Society for Technology Education. Eugene Oregon, 2014.

Holtz-Eakin, Douglas, and Tom Lee. "Projecting Future Skill Shortages through 2029." American Action Forum. July 18, 2019, https://www.americanactionforum.org/research/projecting-future-skill-s.

Hooker, Sarah. "Addressing a Major Barrier to Dual Enrollment Strategies to Staff Up and Scale Up." Jobs for the Future. March 2019. https://files.eric.ed.gov/fulltext/ED598308.pdf.

Hoover, Wesley A. "The Practice Implications of Constructivism." *SEDL Letter* IX, no. 3 (1996).

Horowitz, Juliana Menasce, RuthIgielnik, and Rakesh Kochhar. "Trends in Income and Wealth Inequality." Pew Research Center. January 9, 2020. https://www.pewresearch.org/social-trends/2020/01/09/trends-in-income-and-wealth-inequality/.

Hughes, Gregory I., and Ayanna K. Thomas. "Retrieval Practice and Verbal Visuospatial Transfer: From Memorization to Inductive Learning." *Journal of Memory and Language* 129 (2023).

"Impact of the Coronavirus Pandemic on Fall Plans for Postsecondary Education." National Center for Education Statistics. 2022. Sciences. https://nces.ed.gov/programs/coe/indicator/tpb.

"Innovating Education and Educating for Innovation: The Power of Digital Technologies and Skills." OECD Center for Educational Research and Innovation. 2016. https://www.oecd.org/education/ceri/GEIS2016-Background-document.pdf.

"Institutions and Programs." U.S. Department of Education. December 3, 2002. https://www2.ed.gov/about/offices/list/ous/international/usnei/us/edlite-institutions-us.html.

"Instructional Environment." National Center on Safe Supportive Learning Environments. Office of Safe and Supportive Schools, U.S. Department of Education. 2022. https://safesupportivelearning.ed.gov/topic-research/environment/instructional-environment.

"In Views of U.S. Democracy, Widening Partisan Divides over Freedom to Peacefully Protest." Pew Research Center. September 2, 2020. https://www.pewresearch.org

/politics/2020/09/02/in-views-of-u-s-democracy-widening-partisan-divides-over-freedom-to-peacefully-protest/.

Irwin, Terence. "Inquiry and Dialectic." In *Aristotle's First Principles*. Oxford Academic, 1990, 26–50.

Jackson, Leah, and Kelly A. Cherwin. "Could 'Quiet Quitting' Spell Trouble for Higher Ed?" Higher Ed Jobs. October 4, 2022. https://www.higheredjobs.com/Articles/articleDisplay.cfm?ID=3204.

James, Chris, Michael Connolly, and Melissa Hawkins. "Reconceptualising and Redefining Educational Leadership Practice." *Theory and Practice* 23, no. 5 (2019): 618–35.

Jones, M. Gail, and Laura Brader-Araje. "The Impact of Constructivism on Education: Language, Discourse, and Meaning. *American Communication Journal 5,* no. 3 (2002): 1–10. 'Team Leader." *Effective Executive* 24, no. 1 (2022): 7–12.

Johnson, Aaron. *Online Teaching with Zoom: A Guide for Teaching and Learning with Video Conference Platforms*. Kindle, 2020.

Johnson, Mark W., and Josh Suskewicz. "Leaders, Do You Have a Clear Vision for the Post-Crisis Future?" *Harvard Business Review*. April 17, 2020. https://hbr.org/2020/04/leaders-do-you-have-a-clear-vision-for-the-post-crisis-future.

Johnson, Steven. "In the Rush to Meet Labour Market Needs, Universities Can't Forget the Human Element." *Times Higher Education*. December 2022. https://www.timeshighereducation.com/campus/rush-meet-labour-market-needs-universities-cant-forget-human-element.

June, Audrey Williams. "Higher Ed's Enrollment Fell Again This Fall, If a Bit More Slowly." *Chronicle of Higher Education*. October 2022. https://www.chronicle.com/article/higher-eds-enrollment-fell-again-this-fall-if-a-bit-more-slowly.

Kamenetz, Anya. "'Panic-gogy': Teaching Online Classes during the Coronavirus Pandemic." National Public Radio. March 2020. https://www.npr.org/2020/03/19/817885991/panic-gogy-teaching-online-classes-during-the-coronavirus-pandemic.

Karp, Melinda Mechur, Maria Cormier, Sarah E. Whitley, Sarah M. Umbarger-Wells, and Alexis Wesaw. "First-Generation Students in Community and Technical Colleges: A National Exploration of Institutional Support Practices." Center for First-Generation Student Success NASPA–Student Affairs Administrators in Higher Education Phase Two Advisory. 2020. https://firstgen.naspa.org/research-and-policy/community-and-technical-college-report.

Keeling, Richard P. "Learning Reconsidered: A Campus-Wide Focus on the Student Experience." National Association of Student Personnel Administrators and American College Personnel Association. 2004. https://www.utep.edu/student-affairs/_Files/docs/Assessment/Learning-Reconsidered.pdf.

Kelderman, Eric. "The Silent Treatment: Why College Presidents Don't Speak Out." *The Chronicle of Higher Education*. July 26, 2022. https://www.chronicle.com/article/the-silent-treatment.

Kellerman, Gabriella Rosen, and Martin E. P. Seligman. "There's a Mental Health Crisis at Work Because Life Is Changing Too Fast." *Time*. January 24, 2023. https://time.com/6249306/work-mental-health-crisis-life-changes/.

Kidman, Rachel, Rachel Margolis, Emily Smith-Greenaway, and Ashton M. Verdery. "Estimates and Projections of COVID-19 and Parental Death in the US." *JAMA Pediatrics* 175, no. 7 (2021): 745–46.

Klein, Alyson. "Tech Struggles during COVID-19 Hurting Students' Ability to Learn, Educators Say." *Education Week*. September 24, 2020. https://www.edweek.org/education/tech-struggles-during-covid-19-hurting-students-ability-to-learn-educators-say/2020/09.

Klein-Collins, Rebecca. "Fueling the Race to Postsecondary Success." The Council for Adult and Experiential Learning (CAEL). March 2010. https://files.eric.ed.gov/fulltext/ED524753.pdf.

Klinger, Mary Beth, and Teresa Coffman. "Building Knowledge through Dynamic Meta-Communication" In *Meta-Communication for Reflective Conversations: Models for Distance Education*. Hershey, PA: IGI Global, 2012.

Knox, Liam, L. "Can High Schoolers Save the Community College?" Inside Higher Ed. November 22, 2022. https://www.insidehighered.com/news/2022/11/22/community-colleges-struggle-dual-enrollment-grows.

Koenig, Rebecca. "Mapping Out a 'Credential as You Go' Movement for Higher Education." EdSurge. May 4, 2021. https://www.edsurge.com/news/2021-05-04-mapping-out-a-credential-as-you-go-movement-for-higher-education.

Kohnke, Lucas, and Benjamin Luke Moorhouse. "Adopting HyFlex in Higher Education in Response to COVID-19: Students Perspectives." *The Journal of Open, Distance and eLearning* 36, no. 3 (2021): 231–44.

Kolb, David A. *Experiential Learning: Experience as the Source of Learning and Development*. Upper Saddle River, New Jersey: Prentice Hall, 1984.

Kolko, Jon. "Wicked Problems: Problems Worth Solving: A Handbook and a Call to Action." Austin TX: Austin Center for Design, 2012.

Kopko, Elizabeth, Jessica Brathwaite, and Julia Raufman. "The Next Phase of Placement Reform: Moving toward Equity-Centered Practice." Center for the Analysis of Postsecondary Readiness. August 2022. https://postsecondaryreadiness.org/next-phase-placement-reform-equity-centered-practice/.

Krupnick, Matt. "More Students Are Dropping Out of College during Covid—And It Could Get Worse." The Hechinger Report. February 10, 2022. https://hechingerreport.org/more-students-are-dropping-out-of-college-during-covid-and-it-could-get-worse/.

Krupnick, Matt. "Students Who Counted on Work-Study Jobs Now Struggle to Pay Their Bills: Pandemic Precautions and Remote Learning Leave Many Students with Less Income to Pay for College." *Washington Post*. October 22, 2020. https://www.washingtonpost.com/local/education/college-work-study-coronavirus/2020/10/21/e70c4f72-131d-11eb-ba42-ec6a580836ed_story.html.

Laurentius de Voltolina. *Henricus de Alemannia con i suoi student*. Second half of 14th century. Painting.7 X 8.6 (inches). https://commons.wikimedia.org/wiki/File:Laurentius_de_Voltolina_001.jpg?_ga=2.57876778.18698870.1671388990-1862814611.1671388990.

Lawson, Benn, and Danny Samson. "Developing Innovation Capability in Organizations: A Dynamic Capabilities Approach." *International Journal of Innovation Management* 5 (2001): 377–400.

Lederer, Alyssa M., Mary T. Hoban, Sarah K. Lipson, Sasha Zhou, and Daniel Eisenberg. "More Than Inconvenienced: The Unique Needs of U.S. College Students during the COVID-19." *Pandemic Health Education & Behavior* 48, no. 1 (2020): 14–19.

"Lighting the Path to Remove Systemic Barriers in Higher Education and Award Earned . . . Postsecondary Credentials through IHFP's Degrees When Due Initiative." Institute for Higher Education Policy (IHEP). May 2022. https://www.ihep.org/publication/lighting-the-path-degrees-when-due/.

Llopis, Glenn. "Leading in a Time of Change: Higher Education in Transition." *Forbes*. November 23, 2022. https://www.forbes.com/sites/glennllopis/2022/11/23/leading-in-a-time-of-change-higher-education-in-transition/?sh=191893f71459.

Ma, Jennnifer, Matea Pender, and Meredith Welch. "Education Pays 2019." College Board. 2019. https://research.collegeboard.org/trends/education-pays/report-archive.

MacDowell, Paula. "Teachers Designing Immersive Learning Experiences for Environmental and Sustainability Education." In *Immersive Education*. Springer, Cham., 2022.

"Machines To 'Do Half of All Work Tasks By 2025.'" BBC. October 21, 2020. https://www.bbc.com/news/business-54622189.

MacKenzie, Trevor. "Bringing Inquiry-Based Learning into Your Class." Edutopia. December 1, 2016. https://www.edutopia.org/article/bringing-inquiry-based-learning-into-your-class-trevor-mackenzie.

Malesic, Jonathan. "The Key to Success in College Is So Simple, It's Almost Never Mentioned." *The New York Times*. January 2023. https://www.nytimes.com/2023/01/03/opinion/college-learning-students-success.html.

Marcus, Jon. "A Handful of Colleges Are Finally Providing Training in a Way Consumers Want It: Fast." The Hechinger Report. December 14, 2021. https://hechingerreport.org/a-handful-of-colleges-are-finally-providing-training-in-a-way-consumers-want-it-fast/.

Marcus, Jon. "A New Way to Help College Students Transfer: Admit Them to Two Schools at Once." The Hechinger Report. June 29, 2022. https://hechingerreport.org/a-new-way-to-help-college-students-transfer-admit-them-to-two-schools-at-once/.

Marcus, Jon. "How Higher Education Lost Its Shine." The Hechinger Report. August 2022. https://hechingerreport.org/how-higher-education-lost-its-shine/.

Marcus, Jon. "Momentum Builds behind a Three-Year Degree to Lower College Costs." *Washington Post*. April 15, 2022. https://www.washingtonpost.com/education/2022/04/15/college-three-year-degree/.

Marshall, John, and M. Adamic. "The Story Is the Message: Shaping Corporate Culture." *Journal of Business Strategy* 31, (2010): 18–23.

Marzano, Robert J. *Designing and Teaching Learning Goals and Objectives: Classroom Strategies That Work*. Denver, CO: Marzano Research Laboratory, 2009.

Masterson, Victoria. "From Medicine Drones to Coral Cleaners: 3 'Jobs of The Future' That Are Already Here." World Economic Forum. May 25, 2022. https://www.weforum.org/agenda/2022/05/robots-help-humans-future-jobs/.

McClure, Kevin R., and Alisa Hicklin Fryar. "The Great Faculty Disengagement." *The Chronicle of Higher Education.* January 19, 2022. https://www.chronicle.com/article/the-great-faculty-disengagement.

McGreal, Rory, and Don Olcott. "A Strategic Reset: Micro-Credentials for Higher Education Leaders." *Smart Learning Environments* 9, no. 9 (2022).

McKeachie, Wilbert, and Marilla Svinicki. *Teaching Tips: Strategies, Research, and Theory for College and University Teachers.* Boston: Houghton Mifflin, 2014.

McKie, Andrew. "Using the Arts and Humanities to Promote a Liberal Nursing Education: Strengths and Weaknesses." *Nurse Education Today* 32, no. 7 (2012): 803–10.

McMillan, David W., and David M. Chavis. "Sense of Community: A Definition and Theory." *Journal of Community Psychology* 14, no. 1 (1986).

McMurtrie, Beth. "The Coronavirus Has Pushed Courses Online. Professors Are Trying Hard to Keep Up." *The Chronicle of Higher Education.* March 20, 2020. https://www.chronicle.com/article/the-coronavirus-has-pushed-courses-online-professors-are-trying-hard-to-keep-up/.

Means, Barbara, Yukie Toyama, Robert Murphy, and Marianne Baki. "The Effectiveness of Online and Blended Learning: A Meta-Analysis of the Empirical Literature." *Teachers College Record* 115, no. 3 (2013): 1–47.

Mehta, Jal, and Sarah Fine. *In Search of Deeper Learning: The Quest to Remake the American High School.* Cambridge MA: Harvard University Press, 2019.

Merriam-Webster Dictionary. "Change." 2022. https://www.merriam-webster.com/dictionary/change.

Meyer, Katharine E., Kelli A. Bird, and Benjamin L. Castleman. "Stacking the Deck for Employment Success: Labor Market Returns to Stackable Credentials." EdWorkingPaper, Annenberg Institute at Brown University, 2022.

"Micro-Credentials." National Education Association. 2022. https://www.nea.org/professional-excellence/professional-learning/micro-credentials.

Milner, Richard H. *Start Where You Are, But Don't Stay There.* Harvard Education Press, 2020.

Moises, Naim. "Fads and Fashion in Economic Reforms: Washington Consensus or Washington Confusion?" International Monetary Fund. October 26, 1999. https://www.imf.org/external/pubs/ft/seminar/1999/reforms/naim.htm.

Moll, Luis C. *Vygotsky and Education: Instructional Implications and Applications of Sociohistorical Psychology.* Cambridge University Press. 1990.

Moody, Josh. "Diversity in College and Why It Matters." *U.S. News Education.* March 31, 2020, https://www.usnews.com/education/best-colleges/articles/diversity-in-college-and-why-it-matters.

Moore, Joi L., Camille Dickson-Deane, and Krista Galyen. "eLearning, Online Learning, and Distance Learning Environments: Are They the Same?" *The Internet of Higher Education* 14, no. 2 (2011): 129–35.

Morona, Amy, Daniel Perez, Emma Folts, and , Ian Hodgson. "We Were the Guinea Pig Generation: How the Pandemic Shaped Current College Freshmen." February 1, 2023. *Open Campus.* https://www.opencampusmedia.org/2023/02/01/we-were-the-guinea-pig-generation-how-the-pandemic-shaped-current-college-freshmen/.

Musgrave, Paul. "The Season of Our Professional Discontent." *The Chronicle of Higher Education.* June 9, 2022. https://www.chronicle.com/article/the-season-of-our-professorial-discontent.

Nadworny, Elissa. "The College Enrollment Drop Is Finally Letting Up. That's the Good News." National Public Radio. October 20, 2022. https://www.npr.org/2022/10/20/1129980557/the-college-enrollment-drop-is-finally-letting-up-thats-the-good-news.

Nelson, Eshe, and Melissa Eddy. "European Central Bank Raises Rates Again as Eurozone Inflation Persists." *The New York Times.* February 2, 2023. https://www.nytimes.com/2023/02/02/business/european-central-bank-interest-rates.html.

NewU. "College That Won't Break the Bank." January 21, 2003. https://newu.university/cost/.

Nickels, William, Jim McHugh, and Susan McHugh. *Understanding Business.* New York: McGraw-Hill, 2015.

"Overview: Spring 2022 Enrollment Estimates." National Student Clearinghouse Research Center. Spring 2022. https://nscresearchcenter.org/wp-content/uploads/CTEE_Report_Spring_2022.pdf.

Parker, Kim. "The Growing Partisan Divide in Views of Higher Education." Pew Research Center. August 19, 2019. https://www.pewresearch.org/social-trends/2019/08/19/the-growing-partisan-divide-in-views-of-higher-education-2/.

Pendleton-Jullian, Ann M., and John Seely Brown. *Design Unbound: Designing for Emergence in a White Water World.* Cambridge, MA: The MIT Press, 2018.

Peter, Markie, and M. Folescu. "Rationalism vs. Empiricism." *The Stanford Encyclopedia of Philosophy.* Fall 2021. https://plato.stanford.edu/archives/fall2021/entries/rationalism-empiricism.

Piaget, Jean. *The Psychology of the Child.* New York: Basic Books, 1972.

Pinsker, Joe. "Republicans Changed Their Mind about Higher Education Really Quickly." *The Atlantic.* August 21, 2019. https://www.theatlantic.com/education/archive/2019/08/republicans-conservatives-college/596497/.

"Policy Brief: Education during COVID-19 and Beyond." United Nations. August 2020. https://www.un.org/development/desa/dspd/wp-content/uploads/sites/22/2020/08/sg_policy_brief_covid-19_and_education_august_2020.pdf.

Polnariev, Bernard A., and Mitchell A. Levy. "#SocialEquityMatters: A Multimodal Approach to Strengthening Student Success through Innovation." In *Bridging Marginality through Inclusive Higher Education. Neighborhoods, Communities, and Urban Marginality.* Singapore: Palgrave Macmillan, 2022.

Porat, Ruth. "Expanding Pathways into Higher Education and the Workforce." Google [blog]. October 29, 2021. https://blog.google/outreach-initiatives/grow-with-google/higher-education-partnerships/.

Powell, Farran, Emma Kerr, and Josh Moody. "12 Ways to Cut Your Textbook Costs." *U.S. News.* August 17, 2021. https://www.usnews.com/education/best-colleges/paying-for-college/slideshows/ways-to-cut-your-textbook-costs.

"Public Viewpoint: COVID-19 Work and Education Survey." Strada Center for Consumer Insights. June 10, 2020. https://www.stradaeducation.org/wp-content/uploads/2020/06/Public-Viewpoint-Report-Week-9.pdf.

"#Realcollege 2021: Basic Needs Insecurity during the Ongoing Pandemic." The Hope Center. March 31, 2021. https://hope.temple.edu/sites/hope/files/media/document/HopeNationalReport2021-22-compressed-compressed.pdf.

Reich, Justin. "To Serve All of Our Students, 'We Have to Do Something Different'" EdSurge. January 2023. https://www.edsurge.com/news/2023-01-10-to-serve-all-of-our-students-we-have-to-do-something-different.

"Research on Dual and Concurrent Enrollment Student Outcomes." National Alliance of Concurrent Enrollment Partnerships (NACEP). https://www.nacep.org/resource-center/research-on-dual-and-concurrent-enrollment-student-outcomes/.

Riba, Michelle B., Preeti N. Malani, Robert D. Ernst, and Sagar V. Parikh. "Mental Health on College Campuses: Supporting Faculty and Staff." *Psychiatric Times.* March 18, 2022. https://www.psychiatrictimes.com/view/mental-health-on-college-campuses-supporting-faculty-and-staff.

Rich, John. "Polling Students to Check Understanding." Edutopia. December 14, 2017. https://www.edutopia.org/article/polling-students-check-understanding/.

Robbins, Stephen P., and Timothy A. Judge. *Organizational Behavior.* Upper Saddle River, NJ: Pearson, 2018.

Rourke, Liam, and Heather Kanuka. "Learning in Communities of Inquiry: A Review of the Literature." *Journal of Distance Education* 23, no. 1 (2009): 19–48.

Sabzalieva, Emma, Eglis Chacón, Bosen Lily Liu, Diana Morales, Takudzwa Mutize, Huong Nguyen, and Jaime Roser Chinchilla. "Thinking Higher and Beyond: Perspectives on the Futures of Higher Education to 2050." United Nations Educational Scientific and Cultural Organization. 2021.

Salman, Javeria. "Can Apprenticeships Help Alleviate Teacher Shortages?" The Hechinger Report. September 2, 2022. https://hechingerreport.org/can-apprenticeships-help-alleviate-teacher-shortages.

Salman, Javeria. "How to Plan for a Future of Education Where Disruption is the Norm." The Hechinger Report. January 5, 2022. https://hechingerreport.org/how-to-plan-for-a-future-of-education-where.

Sankey, Michael. "Putting the Pedagogic Horse in Front of the Technology Cart." *Journal of Distance Education in China* 5 (2020): 46–53.

Saul, Stephanie. "At N.Y.U., Students Were Failing Organic Chemistry. Who Was to Blame?" *The New York Times.* October 3, 2022. https://www.nytimes.com/2022/10/03/us/nyu-organic-chemistry-petition.html.

Saul, Stephanie. "College Enrollment Drops, Even as the Pandemic's Effects Ebb." *The New York Times,* May 26, 2022. https://www.nytimes.com/2022/05/26/us/college-enrollment.html.

Schmelke, Sylvia. "Recognizing and Overcoming Inequity in Education." *United Nations Chronicle*. January 22, 2020. https://www.un.org/en/un-chronicle/recognizing-and-overcoming-inequity-education.

Schroeder, Doris, Kate Chatfield, Michelle Singh, Roger Chennells, and Peter Heissone-Kelly.

"The Four Values Framework: Fairness, Respect, Care and Honesty." In *Equitable Research Partnerships*. Springer, Cham., 2019.

Schroeder, Ray. "Higher Ed Curricula – The Short Game." Inside Higher Ed. October 2022. https://www.insidehighered.com/digital-learning/blogs/online-trending-now/higher-ed-curricula%E2%80%94-short-game.

Schroeder, Ray. "Imagine We Are Starting a University Now." Inside HigherEd. September 21, 2022. https://www.insidehighered.com/digital-learning/blogs/online-trending-now/imagine-we-are-starting-university-now.

Schroeder, Ray. "A Second Demographic Cliff Adds to Urgency for Change." Inside HigherEd. May 2021. https://www.insidehighered.com/digital-learning/blogs/online-trending-now/second-demographic-cliff-adds-urgency-change.

Schubert, Emery. "Creativity Is Optimal Novelty and Maximum Positive Affect: A New Definition Based on the Spreading Activation Model." *Frontiers Neuroscience* (2021). 15:612379.

Schwartz, Natalie. "Are More College Closures Ahead?" Higher Ed Dive. April 1, 2021. https://www.highereddive.com/news/are-more-college-closures-ahead/597746/.

Schwartz, Natalie. "Workforce Development, K–12 Teacher Shortages Top List of State Higher Ed Leaders' Concerns." Higher Ed Dive. January 20, 2023. https://www.highereddive.com/news/workforce-development-k-12-teacher-shortages-top-concerns-state-higher-ed-leaders/640805/.

Schwartz, Sarah. "How to Make Teaching Better: 8 Lessons Learned from Remote and Hybrid Learning." *Education Week*. April 20, 2021. https://www.edweek.org/teaching-learning/how-to-make-teaching-better-8-lessons-learned-from-remote-and-hybrid-learning/2021/04.

Selingo, Jeffrey. "Colleges Are Deeply Unequal Workplaces." *The Atlantic*. August 1, 2020. https://www.theatlantic.com/ideas/archive/2020/08/colleges-are-deeply-unequal-workplaces/614791/.

Shulman, Lee. "Those Who Understand: Knowledge Growth in Teaching." *Educational Researcher* 12, no. 2 (1986): 4–14.

Siemens, George. "Learning and Knowing in Networks: Changing Roles for Educators and Designers." *FORUM for Discussion* (2008): 1–26.

Simpson, Zachary. "Reimagining Higher Education in the Wake of COVID-19. *Scholarship of Teaching and Learning in the South* 4, n. 1 (2020): 1–3.

Smith, Barbara Leigh, and Jean T. MacGregor. "What Is Collaborative Learning?" In *Collaborative Learning: A Sourcebook for Higher Education*. National Center on Postsecondary Teaching, Learning, and Assessment at Pennsylvania State University, 1982.

Smith, Brad. "America Faces a Cybersecurity Skills Crisis: Microsoft Launches National Campaign to Help Community Colleges Expand the Cybersecurity

Workforce." Microsoft [blog]. October 28, 2021. https://blogs.microsoft.com/blog/2021/10/28/america-faces-a-cybersecurity-skills-crisis-microsoft-launches-national-campaign-to-help-community-colleges-expand-the-cybersecurity-workforce/.

Sorcinelli, Mary Deane. "Research Findings on the Seven Principles." In *Applying the Seven Principles for Good Practice in Undergraduate Education.* New Directions for Teaching and Learning, no. 47. San Francisco: Jossey-Bass, 1991, 13–25.

Spronken-Smith, Rachel. "Experiencing the Process of Knowledge Creation: The Nature and Use of Inquiry-Based Learning in Higher Education." *International Colloquium on Practices for Academic Inquiry University of Otago* (2012): 1–17.

Stachowiak, Bonni. "Teaching In Higher Ed." *Podcast.* 2023. https://teachinginhighered.com/episodes/.

St. Amour, Madeline. "Greater Need for Food at Community Colleges." Inside Higher Ed. January 7, 2021. https://www.insidehighered.com/news/2021/01/07/community-colleges-see-demand-food-bank-services-swell.

Stauffer, Bri. "What Are 21st Century Skills? Applied Educational Systems (AES)." January 19, 2022. https://www.aeseducation.com/blog/what-are-21st-century-ski.

Steele, Keely, and Lovely Singh. "Combining the Best of Online and Face-to-Face Learning: Hybrid and Blended Learning Approach for COVID-19, Post Vaccine, and Post-Pandemic World." *Journal of Educational Technology Systems* 50. no. 2. (2021): 140–71.

Stein, Ruth Federman, and Sandra Hurd. *Using Student Teams in the Classroom: A Faculty Guide.* Bolton, MA: Anker Publishing, 2000.

Stern, Julie, Krista Ferraro, Kayla Duncan, and Trevor Aleo. *Learning That Transfers: Designing Curriculum for a Changing World.* Thousand Oaks, CA: Corwin, 2021.

"Strengthening Trust in Focus." Aspen Global Leadership Network. 2023. https://www.aspeninstitute.org/programs/aspen-global-leadership-network/.

Squires, David A., William G. Huitt, and John K. Segars. "Improving Classrooms and Schools: What's Important." *Educational Leadership* 39, no. 3: (1981): 174–79.

Sweett, Stephen. "7 Technology and IT Challenges in Higher Education." University Business. December 17, 2020. https://universitybusiness.com/7-technology-and-it-challenges-in-higher-education/.

T. Laura. "10 Of the Oldest Universities in The World." Top Universities.com. December 2022. https://www.topuniversities.com/blog/10-oldest-universities-world.

Tankersley, Jim, and Alan Rappeport. "America Hit Its Debt Limit, Setting Up Bitter Fiscal Fight." *The New York Times.* January 19, 2023. https://www.nytimes.com/2023/01/19/us/politics/debt-limit-economy.html.

Teräs, Marko, Juha Suoranta, Hanna Teräs, and Mark Curcher. "Post-COVID-19 Education and Education Technology 'Solutionism': A Seller's Market." *Postdigital Science and Education* 2 (2020): 863–78.

"The 2020 Annual Homeless Assessment Report (AHAR) to Congress." U.S. Department of Housing and Urban Development Office of Community Planning and Development. January 2021. https://www.huduser.gov/portal/sites/default/files/pdf/2020-AHAR-Part-1.pdf.

"The Global Social Mobility Report 2020." World Economic Forum. January 2020. https://www3.weforum.org/docs/Global_Social_Mobility_Report.pdf.

"The Purpose of Higher Education Part 1." The Change Leader. January 24, 2023. https://changinghighered.com/the-purpose-of-higher-education-part-1/.

"The UDL Guidelines" CAST, 2022, https://udlguidelines.cast.org/.

Thomas, Douglas, and John Seely Brown. "A New Culture of Learning: Cultivating the Imagination for a World of Constant Change" Self-published, CreateSpace, 2011.

"To Achieve Equity in Education." The National Equity Project. 2022. https://www.nationalequityproject.org/.

"Top 11 Skills Employers Look for in Job Candidates," Indeed, October 27, 2022, Retrieved from https://www.indeed.com/career-advice/resumes-cover-letters/skills-employers-look-for.

Torpey, Elka. "Education Pays, 2020." U.S. Bureau of Labor Statistics *Career Outlook*. June 2021. https://www.bls.gov/careeroutlook/2021/data-on-display/education-pays.htm.

"Trends in College Pricing 2018." College Board Trends in Higher Education Series. 2018. https://research.collegeboard.org/media/pdf/trends-college-pricing-2018-full-report.pdf.

Trust, Torrey, Jeffrey P. Carpenter, Daniel G. Krutka, and Royce Kimmons. "#RemoteTeaching and #RemoteLearning: Educator Tweeting during the COVID-19 Pandemic." *Journal of Technology and Teacher Education* 28, no. 2 (2020): 151–59.

Tu, Chih-Hsiung, and Michael Corry. "Building Active Online Interaction via a Collaborative Learning Community." *Computers in Schools. Computers in the Schools* 20, no. 3 (2003): 51–59.

"Undergraduate Retention and Graduation Rates. Condition of Education." U.S. Department of Education Institute of Education Sciences National Center for Education Statistics. 2022. https://nces.ed.gov/programs/coe/indicator/ctr.

"UNESCO COVID-19 Education Response: How Many Students Are at Risk of Not Returning to School? Advocacy Paper." UNESCO: United Nations Educational, Scientific and Cultural Organization. 2020.

Uzgalis, William. "John Locke," The Stanford Encyclopedia of Philosophy, Stanford University. 2022. https://plato.stanford.edu/entries/locke/.

Vaughan, Norman D., Martha Cleveland-Innes, and D. Randy Garrison, *Teaching in Blended Learning Environments: Creating and Sustaining Communities of Inquiry*. Edmonton, AB: AU Press, Athabasca University, 2013.

Vessels, Gordon. "The Creative Process: An Open-Systems Conceptualization." *Journal of Creative Behavior* 16 (1982): 185–96.

Vygotsky, Lev S. *Mind and Society*. Cambridge, MA: Harvard University Press, 1978.

Walls, Helen L. "Wicked Problems and a 'Wicked' Solution." *Global Health* 14, no. 34. (2018).

Wehmeyer, Michael, and Yong Zhao. *Teaching Students to Become Self-Determined Learners*. Alexandria, VA: Association for Curriculum and Development, 2020.

Weill, Peter, Mani Subramani, and Marianne Broadbent. "Building IT Infrastructure for Strategic Agility." October 15, 2002. https://sloanreview.mit.edu/article/building-it-infrastructure-for-strategic-agility/.

"What Is a Makerspace?" 2022. https://www.makerspaces.com/what-is-a-makerspace/.

"What Is Inquiry-Based Learning? Types, Benefits, Examples." SplashLearn. February 9, 2023. https://www.splashlearn.com/blog/what-is-inquiry-based-learning-a-complete-overview/.

"What Is the PESTLE Analysis? An Important Business Analysis Tool." Pestle Analysis. January 1, 2023. https://pestleanalysis.com/what-is-pestle-analysis/.

"What You Need to Know about Higher Education." UNESCO. January 16, 2023. https://www.unesco.org/en/higher-education/need-know#:~:text=Higher%20education%20is%20a%20rich,meet%20ever%20changing%20labour%20markets.

"WHO Coronavirus (COVID-19) Dashboard." World Health Organization. 2023. https://covid19.who.int/.

Whitford, Emma. "A New Push to Create a 3-Year Degree Option." Inside Higher Ed. November 9, 2021. https://www.insidehighered.com/news/2021/11/09/colleges-explore-new-three-year-bachelor%E2%80%99s-degree-program.

Wiggins, Grant P., and Jay McTighe. *Understanding by Design*. Alexandra, VA: Association for Supervision and Curriculum Development, 2005.

Williams, Brittani, Jinann Bitar, Portia Polk, Andre Nguyen, Gabriel Montague, Carrie Gillispie Antoinette, Waller, Azeb Tadesse, and Kayla Elliott. "Student Parent Affordability." *The Education Trust*. August 2022. https://edtrust.org/wp-content/uploads/2014/09/For-Student-Parents-The-Biggest-Hurdles-to-a-Higher-Education-Are-Cost-and-Finding-Child-Care-August-2022.pdf.

Wilson, Donella. "Strategies for Nonprofit Success in a Post-Pandemic Landscape." *Philanthropy News Digest*. June 4, 2021. https://philanthropynewsdigest.org/features/the-sustainable-nonprofit/strategies-for-nonprofit-success-in-a-post-pandemic-landscape.

Wolpert-Gawron, Heather. "What the Heck Is Service Learning?" Edutopia. November 7, 2016. https://www.edutopia.org/blog/what-heck-service-learning-heather-wolpert-gawron.

Wood, Patrick, and Mary Louise Kelly. "'Everybody Is Cheating': Why This Teacher Has Adopted an Open ChatGPT Policy." National Public Radio. January 26, 2023. https://www.npr.org/2023/01/26/1151499213/chatgpt-ai-education-cheating-classroom-wharton-school.

"World Economic Forum Report." World Economic Forum. September 7, 2022. https://www.weforum.org/reports/annual-report-2021-2022.

Wu, Ashley, Enid Chung Roemer, Karen B. Kent, David W. Ballard, and Ron Z. Goetzel. "Organizational Best Practices Supporting Mental Health in the Workplace." *Journal of Occupational and Environmental Medicine* 63, no. 12 (2021).

Youn, Soo. "America's Workers Are Exhausted and Burned Out – and Some Employers Are Taking Notice." *The Washington Post*. June 29, 2021. https://www.washingtonpost.com/business/2021/06/28/employee-burnout-corporate-america/.

Xu, Di, John Fink, and Sabrina Solanki. "College Acceleration for All? Mapping Racial/Ethnic Gaps in Advanced Placement and Dual Enrollment Participation." *American Educational Research Journal* 58, no. 5 (2021): 954–92.

Zalaznick, Matt. "COVID Layoffs, Furloughs Begin Hitting Colleges Hard." *University Business*. July 21, 2020. https://universitybusiness.com/covid-layoffs-furloughs-begin-hitting-colleges-hard/.

Zhao, Yong, and Jim Watterston. "The Changes We Need: Education Post COVID-19." *Journal of Educational Change* 22 (2021): 3–12.

About the Authors

Mary Beth Klinger is a professor in the business department of the School of Professional and Technical Studies at the College of Southern Maryland in La Plata, Maryland. She teaches courses in business, management, strategy, organizational behavior, leadership, small business, marketing, and social entrepreneurship. Her research is focused on organizational innovation and change, as well as community and connectedness. She is passionate about utilizing creative teaching methodologies in her classroom to transform the learning process.

Teresa Coffman is a professor in the College of Education at the University of Mary Washington in Fredericksburg, Virginia. She teaches graduate and undergraduate students in general education courses such as curriculum, instruction, and classroom management, which include theory, methods, culturally responsive teaching, and foundations. She is an expert in the integration of technology throughout the curriculum and has written extensively about inquiry. Her research interests include inquiry-oriented teaching and learning, global and community-based education with an equity-minded focus, and innovation in education.

www.ingramcontent.com/pod-product-compliance
Lightning Source LLC
Chambersburg PA
CBHW032028230426
43671CB00005B/230